W9-CBK-007

Selections from

TENNYSON

Edited by

H. M. BURTON

HUTCHINSON EDUCATIONAL

HUTCHINSON EDUCATIONAL LTD
178-202 Great Portland Street, London W1

London Melbourne Sydney
Auckland Bombay Toronto
Johannesburg New York

★

First published 1960
Reprinted 1962
Reprinted 1963
Reprinted 1964

This book has been set in Fournier type face. It has been printed in Great Britain by William Clowes and Sons Ltd, London and Beccles, on Smooth Wove paper and bound by them

HUTCHINSON ENGLISH TEXTS

Selections from Tennyson

HUTCHINSON ENGLISH TEXTS

Measure for Measure	Edited by James Winny
Troilus and Cressida	Edited by James Winny
Selected Poems of George Herbert	Edited by Douglas Brown
Selections from Tennyson	Edited by H. M. Burton
Three Tales from Conrad	Edited by Douglas Brown
Selected Poetry and Prose of Robert Graves	Edited by James Reeves
W. H. Auden: A Selection	Edited by Richard Hoggart
Selections from Shelley's Poetry and Prose	Edited by Dennis Welland
Viewpoint: An Anthology of Poetry	Edited by Robin Skelton
Andrew Marvell: Some Poems	Edited by James Winny
Edward Thomas: Selected Poems	Edited by Robin Skelton
A Preface to Bacon	Edited by C. J. Dixon
Anthology of Modern Poetry	Edited by John Wain
The Tempest	Edited by James Winny

ACKNOWLEDGEMENT

For permission to reprint six lines from Dante's *Divine Comedy* in Miss Dorothy Sayers' translation, the editor is indebted to Penguin Books Ltd.

Contents

Editorial Note

I AM ALL too conscious of the omissions in this selection—no *Dream of Fair Women*, a mere two hundred lines of *In Memoriam*, nothing of *Maud*, and so on. On the other hand I suspect that some may regard the inclusion of certain poems as whimsical, if not perverse. Within the limits necessarily imposed, however, I have tried to present as many as possible of the 'divers tones' in which Tennyson sang.

For the most part, the notes at the foot of the page are meant to facilitate quick appreciation, and to avoid that break in continuity which comes of much turning of pages and consulting of dictionaries. I have kept critical comment to the minimum, believing that every reader is, or should be, himself a critic; but the Notes at the end of the selection may help to place some of the poems in their context, and to provide a little useful background information.

The order of the poems and the text here used are those of the popular *Works*, first issued by Macmillan in 1894 and many times reprinted. They may be regarded as having the approval of the poet himself since they were based on editions published within his lifetime.

H. M. B.

Introduction

THE FACTS of Tennyson's life are soon stated. He was born at Somersby Rectory in Lincolnshire in 1809, the fourth of twelve children. He attended Louth Grammar School for a few years, but left when he was eleven. At eighteen he published, in collaboration with two of his brothers, *Poems by Two Brothers* (it should have been *Three Brothers*). When he was nineteen he went to Trinity College, Cambridge, and came down three years later without taking a degree. Further volumes of poems were published in 1832, 1842, 1847 (*The Princess*) and 1850 (*In Memoriam*). In this year, 1850, he also married and became Poet Laureate. From 1850 to his death in 1892 there is nothing to record except the publication of many more volumes, various changes of address, and his acceptance of a peerage in 1883. Few great men—and despite certain opinions to the contrary it is generally accepted that Tennyson *was* a great man—have lived for eighty-three years and, apart from publishing a score of volumes of poems and plays, done so little in that time.

Yet despite the apparent eventlessness of his life, Tennyson was an unusual and fascinating character. For one thing, he was the last great poet to devote his life entirely to poetry. Certain lesser writers of verse, in his day and since, have caught the popular taste and made a comfortable income for a time; but their names and their verses are now almost forgotten. Tennyson not only caught the popular taste and made a great deal of money with his pen; he happened also to be a great poet who is still loved and remembered.

Moreover, the bare facts and dates set out above, if they seem

1*

to suggest a dull and uninteresting life, merely reflect Tennyson's own attitude to what nowadays we should call publicity. He held firmly to the belief that a man's private life is his own affair; nothing would have pleased him more than to know that these few facts and figures were the sum total of information to be divulged. Unfortunately, if we are to understand and appreciate him fully, we cannot leave it at that—and in any case the biographers have been busy. Many detailed *Lives*—one by his own son—have been written round those few facts, and some of them have been very big books indeed. His life may have been outwardly uneventful, yet there is scarcely a single fact known about it which does not, with a little intelligent study, reveal something of vital importance to our appreciation of Tennyson as a poet, and as a man.

Take, for example, his birthplace—Somersby Rectory. Somersby is a tiny village in the Lincolnshire Wolds—gently-rounded and wooded hills in what is often thought to be a flat and featureless county. It is still completely rural. It has a small stream and it is not far from the sea. In fine weather it is a delectable place, but it can be grey and cold and inhospitable. The farmers and the fishermen in this part of the world can be grim and 'close'; they are still comparatively unsophisticated and uncommunicative, but they have the old virtues of loyalty, family affection, industry and simple religion. . . . And there is nothing in this paragraph about Somersby which does not find expression somewhere or other in Tennyson's poetry.

Next, Somersby *Rectory*. The word 'Rectory' tells us a great deal. When we learn that Dr Tennyson, the poet's father, was a disappointed man, who was given two or three livings as a consolation for being disinherited in favour of a younger brother; when we learn that he was primarily a scholar who had no real vocation for the Church but who did his duty faithfully and well all his life; when we read that he was a man given to fits of deep depression which sometimes affected the whole family—when we know all this we begin to guess something of life beneath the surface at that crowded Rectory.

But that is only the beginning. In the nineteenth century there were very few country clergymen who were not members of substantial families, families who could afford to send their sons to the Universities. Despite his eleven children (one died in infancy), Dr Tennyson could send his oldest boy to Eton and his first three sons to Cambridge; and when Alfred came down there was never any question of his getting some kind of paid employment. He went visiting friends or he hung about at home. Who kept him, one wonders? Who—not to mince matters—paid for his tobacco, for his friendly drinks with neighbouring squires and farmers and fishermen, for his clothes, for his fares? Obviously there was money in the family; the point is that the young Tennyson never knew poverty.

This is more important than it may at first seem. Poets are sensitive souls, and Tennyson was no exception. He was supremely sensitive, for example, to the sounds and sights of nature; he had an exquisitely sensitive ear for lyrical poetry; he was sensitive, too, to the appeal of the obvious virtues like loyalty and patriotism. Yet there seem to be whole tracts and regions of simple humanity to which he was to all intents and purposes completely blind. He lived, for example, through the period when Italy, Greece, Spain, Belgium and other countries were striving with varying success to throw off the yoke of unenlightened subjection; yet apart from a fruitless journey to Spain in his youth (which we shall record later) and a few references to the struggles of Poland and of Montenegro, to which his attention was specifically drawn, there is nothing in his poetry to suggest that he had any sympathy with the enslaved. The war in the United States to determine the future of slavery aroused in him no enthusiasm. For France, the home of liberty and the nurse of civilisation and culture, he had nothing but suspicion and often harsh words. Nearer home, the efforts of the poor to win an improvement in their lot received no encouragement; too often, in fact, the poor were noble and loyal in his eyes if they accepted their fate and did their duty, but became 'lawless mobs' when they attempted to rise above it. He seriously believed that 'great men' alone could bring about the millennium, and even for their effect he seemed content to allow a thousand years or so of good steady government along well established lines.

One has only to think of the passionate rebelliousness of Byron, of Shelley, of the young Wordsworth, and, indeed, even of Coleridge to appreciate this great deficiency in Tennyson both as a man and as a poet; and it is not too far-fetched an argument to suggest that this particular insensitiveness may have been due, at least in part, to his comfortable childhood and youth. If he had known what it was to be hungry or to sleep cold; if he had not been able to spend three pleasant years at Cambridge without even the necessity of working for a degree; if he had had to go to work in some dusty solicitor's office or some crowded city classroom—then perhaps he might have widened the scope of his love and sympathy for mankind as a whole.

Nor is it unlikely that his comfortable and sheltered life was responsible for a certain discomfort and unease when dealing with real (as opposed to fictitious and ideal) men and women, which was a part of his make-up both as a man and as a poet. If we except his sketches of a few Lincolnshire characters and some of his least ambitious rural idylls, there is scarcely a portrait of a man or a woman in his pages which will stand up for a moment—as far as simple 'human-ness' goes—to the least of Browning's creations, for instance. This inability to create people of flesh and blood cramped his efforts to succeed in a field where he strove mightily, but vainly, for years—the theatre. His plays have a few fine scenes and much glorious poetry? but they seldom come to life on the stage because their characters seldom come to life either.

But Somersby Rectory was not the only formative influence of young Alfred's boyhood. At the age of seven—in those far-off days before Education Acts and examinations—he entered the grammar school in the neighbouring town of Louth. It was run by a fierce schoolmaster who believed in the Classics and the cane. Tennyson, who lodged with his grandmother, was bitterly unhappy and left when he was eleven. He lost nothing educationally, as his father was a scholar who had a large library and who conscientiously taught his children. When he was still only twelve, the lad was writing a long and learned letter to his aunt in Louth devoted entirely to a critical appreciation of Milton's *Samson Agonistes*. But book-learning is not all, even in a poet's make-up. Five or six years at a good school might have done much to round off and expand his personality; they might even have made him a better mixer and given him a sense of humour. There are many accounts of him which suggest that, as a man, he had a fund of entertaining stories; but it is strange that none of these stories has been handed down. In any case a sense of humour is something more than the gift for telling an amusing tale; if Tennyson had possessed it, surely somewhere in his vast output of verse there would be something to suggest so.

In fact there are just as many accounts which reveal a complete absence of that subtlety, and sense of proportion, which are the essence of humour. The following anecdotes, for example, may be completely fictitious; the second in particular was not related until many years after Tennyson's death. Their importance lies in the fact that he must have been the sort of person about whom such stories could plausibly have been invented—if they were invented. When he was old and famous he was much plagued by sightseers, who would hang about the lanes round his house in the hope of catching a glimpse of him. On one occasion some tourists caught him unawares at his own gate, and are said to have asked him a favour—a few minutes' conversation, perhaps, or even his autograph. The Great Man fled into his house, his romantic cloak flying behind him, muttering (so it is reported): 'No, no. It cannot be.' If that was what he really did and said, one can only marvel at his apparent pompousness and complete lack of humour. There is an even more amazing story of when he was older still and yet more famous. It was at a garden-party—the kind of function which he normally shunned, and at which he was supremely unhappy. He had found an empty seat in a secluded corner and was sitting alone with his thoughts, when his retreat was discovered by a pretty young woman, a devout disciple but, quite understandably, terribly shy. Tennyson was far too polite to get up immediately and walk off, but he gave the stranger no encouragement. Eventually she leaned forward to speak to him. As she did so the Great Man turned to her as she sat beside him on the seat and said, very seriously, 'Madam, your stays creak.' The young lady was shocked and fled. An hour or two later a mildly distressed Lord Tennyson was seen wandering among the guests, peering into the faces of the young ladies (his sight was notoriously weak). At last he found the one he was looking for, stood before her and raised his hat. 'Madam,' he said, 'I apologise. It was my braces.'

But this is to anticipate. We left young Tennyson at the age of twelve, having finished his short schooling, writing a scholarly letter to the aunt who had invited him to send her 'remarks on works and authors'. For the next six years we know little about him. He studied Greek and Latin with his father, he visited his relations in other parts of Lincolnshire, and every summer he went with the family for a sea-side holiday at Mablethorpe. And all the time he read—all the English classics and many of the French—and wrote poetry. He seems to have made up his mind from a very early age that he would be a poet, and his understanding parents did nothing to discourage him.

Of *Poems by Two Brothers* it is only necessary to say that Tennyson, as an old man, called his share in it his 'early rot' and 'could hardly tolerate it'. The anonymous poets received £20 for their efforts—a surprisingly large sum, incidentally; it would be equal to at least £100 today. But they had to take a good part of it in books from the bookseller who was also the publisher; with some of the rest Charles and Alfred hired a carriage and drove the fourteen miles into Mablethorpe 'to share their triumph with the winds and waves'.

In February, 1828, the two brothers Charles and Alfred entered Trinity College, Cambridge, Frederick having preceded them there in 1827. It seems nowadays a strange date to have chosen—about the middle of the middle term of the academic year. But since the obtaining of a degree seems not to have been the main object of Tennyson's university education, presumably the date of admission was immaterial. It may even have been delayed somewhat by his father's stern refusal to allow his son to go to Cambridge until he had recited, on two successive evenings, the whole of the *Odes* of Horace.

Cambridge was an important factor in the making of the poet. He was soon a member of a sort of informal club, known as the Apostles, which read and discussed each other's essays on 'mind and art', on the soul, on economics and politics, on religion and on anything else that took their fancy. He was one of the most silent members, however; shy, handsome, enormous, sitting in a corner taking notes. The others were nearly all men who achieved distinction later in some profession or other. To the boy from the sheltered, scholarly, country Rectory, Cambridge must have been a wonderfully revealing experience. When he left in February 1831, because his father was not well and wanted Alfred at home to help his mother, he was a man, with two valuable achievements behind him. The first was his book, *Poems, Chiefly Lyrical*, which had been well reviewed and had appeared while he was still an undergraduate of 21; the other was something he was to regard as the greatest achievement of his life: he had won the love and friendship of Arthur Henry Hallam.

Hallam is almost like one of those characters sometimes

encountered in a play, who seem to exist only in other people's minds. They never appear on the stage, so we never meet them; yet they are always being spoken of, and they occasionally have an important influence on the characters whom we do meet. Tennyson was not the only one to regard him as exceptionally gifted and charming. At Eton he outshone Gladstone, who honoured him all his long life, and mourned him as an irreplaceable loss to philosophy and theology. At Cambridge he was hailed as the great statesman of the future. Of all the Apostles he was the most versatile; the quickest thinker; the shrewdest critic—and the gayest companion. Unfortunately there is very little to support these impressive opinions: the character hardly appears in person, and we have to accept the word of his admirers. There are some letters from him, and a handful of short poems and essays. The letters are affectionate, and the poems and essays are cultured and scholarly. But there is little to suggest the almost perfect young man so deeply loved and admired by all who ever knew him.

However, there can be little doubt that Tennyson's friendship with Hallam was one of the major events of his life. With Hallam he travelled to Spain to carry funds to certain rebels whose gallant stand against tyranny had greatly impressed the Apostles. (The insurrection failed.) After Tennyson had left Cambridge and his father had died, Hallam was a frequent visitor to Somersby, where the new Rector had allowed the Tennysons to go on living in the Rectory. They had long walks and talks, and Hallam became engaged to Tennyson's sister Emily. Together the two friends visited Cologne and the Rhine; together they saw Tennyson's next volume, *Poems*, through the press (1832). The almost daily contact with such a rare spirit raised the young poet to the heights (even while some unfavourable criticisms of his latest book plunged him into the depths); and Hallam's engagement to his sister seemed to provide just that link of certainty which would bind the two friends together for all time.

And then suddenly Hallam died. He was in Vienna with his father when, without even a hint or a warning, he collapsed on a couch and died of a broken blood-vessel.

This would have been a cruel blow in any circumstances; its suddenness and unexpectedness made it even heavier—and not for poor Tennyson alone. Among those who mourned Hallam was Emily Tennyson, who was seriously ill for months. Years afterwards the poet told his son that the blow had, 'for a while, blotted out all joy from his life, and made him long for death'.

The immediate (or comparatively immediate) result of his grief was a poem called at first *Thoughts of a Suicide*, but eventually published as *The Two Voices*; in this the stricken soul argues at length with his other self on the rightness and wrongness of suicide. It is not now very easy or lively reading, but there are genuine cases of men who have been deterred from taking their own lives by close reading of this poem. The *ultimate* result of Tennyson's grief was *In Memoriam*, but although this was begun in 1834 it was not finished or published until 1850.

For a great man, and a man of high soul, Tennyson was all his life sensitive to adverse criticism. One or two notices of his *Poems* (1832) were unfavourable, and he was so upset that he published nothing more for ten years. At one time, indeed, he seriously contemplated leaving a country where he was obviously not appreciated; but he felt it his duty to stay and look after the family, both his older brothers having left home. What pained him most, to do him justice, was that he realised the force of some of the criticisms. His next ten years were not spent sulking in silence. He revised and reconstructed many of the 1832 poems; he was always writing new ones; and he drew up for himself a stiff weekly time-table of 'homework' which included German on five days in the week, the sciences, and (in the evenings) poetry. (How closely he stuck to it is not recorded.)

But as the years went by he recovered, naturally enough, from the first overwhelming shock. He visited friends in Surrey; when the new Rector finally required Somersby Rectory, Tennyson supervised the family's move to a house in Epping Forest (in 1837), to Tunbridge Wells (1840) and to Boxley, near Maidstone (in 1841); he went to London more frequently, and met old friends and new. Among the latter was Carlyle, who has left a striking pen-portrait of him: 'a man solitary and sad, as certain men are, dwelling in an element of gloom. . . . One of the finest looking men in the world. A great shock of rough dusky dark hair; bright laughing hazel eyes; massive aquiline face, most massive yet most delicate; of sallow brown complexion, almost Indian looking, clothes cynically loose, free-and-easy, smokes infinite tobacco. . . .'

Then in 1842 appeared *Poems, by Alfred Tennyson*, in two volumes. A second edition appeared the next year, a third in 1845, a fourth in 1846—and so on, until there were enough new poems to make a completely new book. In short, the two-volume edition was a success—and no wonder! It contained the best of the 1832 poems, many of them revised and some of them almost entirely re-written, as well as such eternal favourites as *Break, Break, Break*, *Ulysses*, and *Locksley Hall*. Tennyson's name was on the lips of all who read poetry, both here and in America.

But apparently not enough people, even in Tennyson's day, read—or at least bought—poetry to keep the wolf from the poet's door. His letters during the next few years are dated from all over the country, from Eastbourne to Killarney, and although he was often staying with friends or relations he must have needed quite an appreciable income for travel. To make matters a great deal worse he invested his whole capital (and some of his brothers' and sisters' capital into the bargain) in a company which was somehow to combine philanthropy with the manufacture of artistic wood-carving. (What *is* it about crackbrained financial schemes which has such a fascination for literary geniuses?) The firm failed completely, and Tennyson lost all his money. Not unnaturally, he fell ill and went to Cheltenham for treatment.

But his salvation was not far off. In 1845 Carlyle, one of his friends, spoke to Lord Houghton, another of his friends, about getting a pension for Tennyson. (It would be a Civil List grant today, but was then called a pension, and was paid from Government funds.) Lord Houghton spoke to Sir Robert Peel, the Prime Minister, and Tennyson duly received his pension of £200 a year. This would be worth at least £1,000 a year today, and however glad one may feel for Tennyson's sake, one cannot help feeling some regret that John Keats, say, or William Blake, or even D. H. Lawrence, never had friends or connections who might have secured some such grant to make life easier and sweeter for struggling genius.

During the next four or five years he visited Switzerland, Ireland, Scotland and Cornwall, made frequent trips to London and continued his cure at Cheltenham. He also published *The Princess*. This went through four editions in five years, each time revised or added to, so it must have been popular; but Carlyle and Edward Fitzgerald (of *Omar Khayyam*) were not being completely flippant when they said that they 'gave up all hopes of him after *The Princess*'. If *lasting* fame is what counts they were right; apart from the songs, *The Princess* is seldom read today.

His *annus mirabilis*, however, was undoubtedly 1850. In May *In Memoriam* was first printed; in June it was published, and Tennyson was married; in November he was made Poet Laureate.

The Laureateship was offered to him (after being declined by Samuel Rogers) on the death of Wordsworth. He fulfilled the duties of the office ably and conscientiously. These no longer included the writing of flattering odes to the Sovereign, but Tennyson seldom let a royal or a national occasion pass without his poetical tribute.

His marriage presents another baffling feature of this strange and fascinating character. He first met Emily Selwood when he was a young man of 21, but saw little of her until 1836 when she was a bridesmaid to her sister, who was marrying Tennyson's brother Charles. If he did not actually fall in love then, he admitted later that he pressed her hand 'and knew the press return'd' (in church, apparently). They corresponded affectionately for four years, but in 1840 the correspondence was terminated abruptly, presumably by Emily's parents, as Alfred had no income and no prospects of ever acquiring one. That Alfred might conceivably buckle to and get a job, so that he might some day be in a position to propose to the girl, seems to have occurred to nobody, least of all to Alfred. Nor is there any indication, at any rate in any of the poet's letters and diaries which his son saw fit to publish after his death, that Alfred ever questioned the parental ban or sought to have it removed. Even when the pension arrived—to set him, surely, beyond the fear of destitution even if he never sold another poem—he still apparently gave no thought to the girl he had loved, and agreed so meekly to give up, six years earlier. And then in 1850 they met again at a friend's house—and one wonders whether the meeting was 'arranged' by a third party. *In Memoriam* had produced an advance of £300 from the publisher and seemed likely to earn more; Emily's father offered them furniture; and within a month or two they were married. But the strange story has a happy ending: Emily was a devoted wife and mother, and Tennyson, many years later, said, 'The peace of God came into my life before the altar when I wedded her.'

In Memoriam, the third great wonder of this wonderful year, is not as it is frequently termed, an epic; it is a collection of 131 lyrics, with a prologue and an epilogue. Some of the lyrics, or 'Elegies', were first written soon after Hallam's death in 1833; nearly all of them before 1842. They had been accumulating in a special note-book ('a long butcher-ledger-like book' was how the poet described it when it was temporarily lost), and had been constantly revised, rewritten, and polished. The fact that they are all in the same stanza form seems to suggest that Tennyson always intended they should be collected and appear as a single work; but their subject-matter varies considerably. There are scenes of Christmas and New Year festivities; sections on semi-theological subjects like reunion after death; others on sleep and dreams; others on scientific thought. It is possible to regard the work in many ways. Some will consider it a record of one man's grief and of his efforts to overcome despair by faith; others (like Arthur Hallam's father) will think of it as a deathless memorial to a young man dead in his prime; but however it is viewed it is impossible not to admire the poet's mastery of his chosen metre, the occasional pictures of the English countryside, the moving eloquence of the mourner, even the intensity of the bereaved friend's efforts to convince himself that there is a world hereafter in which parted souls will be reunited. It was this aspect of the poem which appealed most strongly to Queen Victoria after the death of the Prince Consort—although she, a less complicated person perhaps, had no doubts to dispel or to defeat. She sent for him and told him that 'next to the Bible, *In Memoriam* was her comfort'. It has been the comfort and inspiration of many less famous mourners since then.

It is not much of an exaggeration to say that there is nothing of importance to record of Tennyson's life after 1850. Things happened to him, of course. He prospered exceedingly; having bought a house and made a home in the Isle of Wight, he had another house built for himself in Surrey, and kept both until he died. (Did he keep the pension? His biographers are silent on the point.) He had two sons, one of whom died when he was thirty-two, the other living to write a monumental *Memoir* of his father. He published many more volumes of poetry, some of which, like *Maud*, were not well received, but most of which, like the *Idylls of the King*, were very popular. He became a peer. From 1865 selections and collections of his work began to appear in all sizes and all types of binding, the *Library Edition* reaching ten volumes in the year of his death. In 1875 he began writing for the stage, but only his last play, *Becket*, had any real success. And in 1892 he died.

Among the poems Tennyson published after 1850 there were, of course, many which bore the marks of greatness; some of them will be found in this collection. There were even some—too long for inclusion here—which revealed *new* marks of greatness; marks which had not appeared in his work before 1850. Some, like *Northern Farmer*, contain the nearest thing to humour in all his work; others, like *The Revenge*, reveal a powerful narrative gift; the *Idylls*, while less successful than one might have expected as narratives, do at least tell a story with more purpose and movement than he had exhibited earlier in his work. And even in the least memorable of his post-1850 work there are lines and lyrics and passages which recall the glorious creative vigour and freshness of his prime.

But for the most part it is the Tennyson of the years before 1850 (and *In Memoriam*, it must be remembered, was written before 1850) whom we most love and admire. Lovers of poetry sometimes amuse themselves by wondering what heights might have been reached by Keats had he lived to be more than twenty-six; with Tennyson the interesting speculation is exactly the opposite: what would have been his reputation as a poet had he died not, indeed, at the age of twenty-six but, say, when he was forty? Not that his decline—and it is not every critic who will admit that it *was* a decline—was in any way exceptional; few poets, even of the highest fame, have retained their greatest powers throughout a long life. Composers and painters seem to grow in greatness of imagination and inspiration almost to the day of their death; poets nearly all reach their peak some time between their thirties and their fifties, and then decline.

What constitutes the greatness of Tennyson at his peak the poems in this selection will reveal; and it is best that each reader should make his own discoveries. A few generalisations, however, may serve as pointers and help the reader to know what to look for. It is convenient to divide such generalisations into those concerned with the matter of his poems, and those concerned with the manner.

To begin with the manner: the most outstanding feature of Tennyson's poetry is its music. A good deal of nonsense is written and talked about the music of poetry, and *music* is at best only a loose metaphorical word for the quality in question. But the root of the matter lies in the fact that poetry is written to be *heard*; even when it is read silently it should be heard in the mind. Tennyson himself read his poetry aloud on every possible occasion to anybody who would sit quiet and listen. Now nearly everything Tennyson wrote *sounds* good; sometimes, indeed, it sounds better than it is! And this effect is not accidental. It may be true that when a poet thinks of words in which to clothe an idea the words that come first to his mind or his pen are more pleasant-sounding than those of an ordinary man; but few poets are content with the words that come first to their minds or pens. They shape them and rearrange them and change them until they are satisfied—if they ever are. In the first inspiration, as in the final version, several factors play their part. There is for example the variety of vowel-sounds. In a single line,

> And at their feet the crocus brake like fire,

there may be seven or eight different vowel-sounds. In most of Tennyson's poetry these vowel-sounds, as they follow each other and are echoed and re-echoed in succeeding lines, make a pleasing sound, or series of sounds, which for want of a better word we call music. It is partly instinct and partly art. Tennyson, for example, would never have been guilty of one of Matthew Arnold's least happy lines,

> Who prop, thou ask'st, in these bad days, my mind?

which, apart from the fact that it is difficult to say, contains a series of unpleasing vowel-sounds. If Tennyson could not clothe the thought he wished to express in words which expressed it more winningly than that, he would have rejected the thought altogether.

Another factor in this music is the so-called *cæsura.* This is a technical term for the pause which is supposed to occur at or near the middle of every metrical line. It is open to question whether there *is* a natural pause there, and it may be that if we had never heard of the cæsura we should never have noticed these pauses! But *if* there is one somewhere in every metrical line then one thing is certain: if that pause occurred at exactly the same spot—dead in the middle—the effect would be more like the ticking of a metronome than the sound of poetry. The subtle shift of the cæsura in succeeding lines of Tennyson's verse is something to look for on the printed page and, better still, to listen for in the spoken poem.

A third element of Tennyson's poetic manner is, unfortunately, more of a mannerism. His education was classical, and the classical poets were much addicted to certain tricks of the trade which have come to be known as *figures of speech*, although they are less common in normal speech than in writing. Some of these, like *simile* and *metaphor*, are familiar; others have never been completely at home in English writing. When Tennyson wrote

> His honour rooted in dishonour stood,
> And faith unfaithful kept him falsely true

he was showing off. He was using a figure called *oxymoron* which in Greek or Latin verse is peculiarly effective, but which in English seems unnatural, strained and affected. Often he used these figures of speech—particularly *onomatopœia*—with astonishing skill; at other times he just as astonishingly failed to realise that he was over-doing it a little. This again is something to look for. Since this is a collection of, on the whole, his better poems, there will be more genuine than spurious beauties to be discovered; the important thing to notice, in any case, is his mastery of poetic artifice—which is perhaps a more dignified term than tricks of the trade. Few poets have so expertly managed to make every consonant and every vowel contribute towards the picture or the sound they wished to suggest. For some people Tennyson's word-painting is a little too rich, too ornate, and sometimes too obvious; others can never have enough of it. There can be no hard and fast rules in such a matter, and each must decide for himself.

When we come to consider those qualities of Tennyson's subject-matter which, at least in his prime, contributed to his greatness, it is difficult to decide on priorities. Many will say that the most important element was the exactness with which he expressed his own times. His Age asked for romantic, colourful poetry, and he supplied it. His Age was beginning to ask questions about man's origins and his ultimate destiny, and if Tennyson did not answer the questions, he too asked them and suggested possible (and not discouraging) solutions to many of the nagging problems raised by scientists and discoverers. His Age was increasingly patriotic, if not jingoistic: he wrote lovingly of the England he so loved; and later was to celebrate English prowess in stirring verses which everybody could enjoy. There were whole tracts of English life about which he knew little and seemed to care not at all; but they were the tracts which most educated people of his time seemed as eager as he to ignore. (When Dickens sent Tennyson a set of his works, 'believing that you have no more earnest and sincere homage than mine', he must surely have done so with mental reservations; their worlds seldom approached each other, let alone touched.) This gift, this power to express the spirit of his age, was but one facet of Tennyson's genius, though many would rank it the highest.

Others would claim that his classical themes and allusions were the most marked of his characteristics. His education, as we have seen, whether at Louth, in his father's study, or at Cambridge, was severely confined to the Greek and Latin authors; everything else he knew he had taught himself in those long years of bachelor solitude at Somersby after young Hallam's death. Certainly, in poems like *Ulysses*, *The Lotos Eaters*, *Œnone* and dozens of others, he seized and interpreted the classical spirit far more satisfactorily than he ever recaptured the mediæval spirit (except perhaps in *The Lady of Shalott*). Even his Arthurian characters are often presented to us more as Virgilian heroes and heroines than as men and women of mediæval Britain. However, for better or for worse, Tennyson's creation of classical atmosphere remains one of the outstanding elements in his make-up.

But for the majority, surely, he stands pre-eminent as a poet of 'nature'. There is scarcely a poem in his vast output which does not somewhere reveal his patient and loving observation of the sounds and sights of natural life. His range covers all seasons, and extends from the smallest creatures to the vastest landscapes (or landskips as he called them). The surprising thing is that we possibly owe a great deal of this richness to his weak eyesight. Extreme short-sightedness can have some unexpected effects. It is said to breed in many victims a marked inferiority complex, and may indeed partly explain Tennyson's shyness. It is even said to have made possible Blondin's amazing feats on the tight-rope![1] It certainly helped Tennyson to become a keen student of nature. To see as much as other people see he had to look very closely and very patiently; and in looking closely he eventually saw *more* than other people see. Moreover his short-sightedness made him more keenly aware than most of us of the sounds of nature. When this habit—part inborn, part self-taught—of devoted observation was applied to his other natural gift, that of finding the best words in the best order, in which to record what he saw and heard, the result was a great body of fascinating 'nature' poetry. Its setting is authentic; usually recognisable as English

[1] When he looked away from his wire he saw nothing, so he was never giddy.

countryside in detail or in outline. The thought may not always be profound but it is always thoroughly sincere and deeply felt. And correctness and sincerity are two of the ingredients necessary for immortality.

As so often happens with writers ecstatically acclaimed by their own contemporaries, Tennyson's reputation suffered a sharp decline soon after his death. His beauties were sneered at as pretty-pretty, or over-elaborate; his ideas were dismissed as shallow and obvious; his sympathies were declared narrow and imperfect. There was some truth in all these strictures, but they were not the whole truth. Over the last few decades there has been a steady re-appraisal of his worth as a poet, and it is now generally acknowledged that with all his faults there was yet a rich core of true poetry in his work, and especially in that which was written before 1850. For students, indeed, he is an ideal poet because he seldom lacks interest. When he is not telling an entertaining story he is painting an entertaining picture—and all in a language which, except for the hopelessly tone-deaf, compels attention because of its variety and its charm. His language is, moreover, seldom obscure or difficult to follow, and his thought seldom too profound. He has often been, and probably will continue to be, 'the plain man's poet'—and in this case the compliment is not a smear. Nothing, in fact, would have given Tennyson greater satisfaction than the thought that, through him, many a 'plain' man has first come to love poetry.

Selections from Tennyson

To the Queen

Revered, beloved—O you that hold
  A nobler office upon earth
  Than arms, or power of brain, or birth
Could give the warrior kings of old,

Victoria,—since your Royal grace   5
  To one of less desert allows
  This laurel greener from the brows
Of him that utter'd nothing base;

And should your greatness, and the care
  That yokes with empire, yield you time   10
  To make demand of modern rhyme
If aught of ancient worth be there;

Then—while a sweeter music wakes,
  And thro' wild March the throstle calls,
  Where all about your palace-walls   15
The sun-lit almond-blossom shakes—

Take, Madam, this poor book of song;
  For tho' the faults were thick as dust
  In vacant chambers, I could trust
Your kindness. May you rule us long,   20

And leave us rulers of your blood
  As noble till the latest day!
  May children of our children say,
'She wrought her people lasting good;

7–8 a reference to the Laureateship and (l. 8) to Wordsworth

'Her court was pure; her life serene;
God gave her peace; her land reposed;
A thousand claims to reverence closed
In her as Mother, Wife, and Queen;

'And statesmen at her council met
Who knew the seasons when to take
Occasion by the hand, and make
The bounds of freedom wider yet

'By shaping some august decree,
Which kept her throne unshaken still,
Broad-based upon her people's will,
And compass'd by the inviolate sea.'

March 1851

Mariana

'Mariana in the moated grange.'

Measure for Measure

WITH blackest moss the flower-plots
Were thickly crusted, one and all:
The rusted nails fell from the knots
That held the pear to the gable-wall.
The broken sheds look'd sad and strange:
Unlifted was the clinking latch;
Weeded and worn the ancient thatch
Upon the lonely moated grange.
She only said, 'My life is dreary,
He cometh not,' she said;
She said, 'I am aweary, aweary,
I would that I were dead!'

27 *closed* joined
30 *the seasons* the right times

Her tears fell with the dews at even;
  Her tears fell ere the dews were dried;
She could not look on the sweet heaven, 15
  Either at morn or eventide.
After the flitting of the bats,
  When thickest dark did trance the sky,
  She drew her casement-curtain by,
And glanced athwart the glooming flats. 20
    She only said, 'The night is dreary,
      He cometh not,' she said;
    She said, 'I am aweary, aweary,
      I would that I were dead!'

Upon the middle of the night, 25
  Waking she heard the night-fowl crow:
The cock sung out an hour ere light:
  From the dark fen the oxen's low
Came to her: without hope of change,
  In sleep she seem'd to walk forlorn, 30
  Till cold winds woke the gray-eyed morn
About the lonely moated grange.
    She only said, 'The day is dreary,
      He cometh not,' she said;
    She said, 'I am aweary, aweary, 35
      I would that I were dead!'

About a stone-cast from the wall
  A sluice with blacken'd waters slept,
And o'er it many, round and small,
  The cluster'd marish-mosses crept. 40
Hard by a poplar shook alway,
  All silver-green with gnarled bark:
  For leagues no other tree did mark
The level waste, the rounding gray.

40 *marish-mosses* marsh-mosses

She only said, 'My life is dreary,
He cometh not,' she said;
She said, 'I am aweary, aweary,
I would that I were dead!'

And ever when the moon was low,
And the shrill winds were up and away,
In the white curtain, to and fro,
She saw the gusty shadow sway.
But when the moon was very low,
And wild winds bound within their cell,
The shadow of the poplar fell
Upon her bed, across her brow.
She only said, 'The night is dreary,
He cometh not,' she said;
She said, 'I am aweary, aweary,
I would that I were dead!'

All day within the dreamy house,
The doors upon their hinges creak'd;
The blue fly sung in the pane; the mouse
Behind the mouldering wainscot shriek'd,
Or from the crevice peer'd about.
Old faces glimmer'd thro' the doors,
Old footsteps trod the upper floors,
Old voices called her from without.
She only said, 'My life is dreary,
He cometh not,' she said;
She said, 'I am aweary, aweary,
I would that I were dead!'

The sparrow's chirrup on the roof,
The slow clock ticking, and the sound
Which to the wooing wind aloof
The poplar made, did all confound

Her sense; but most she loathed the hour
When the thick-moted sunbeam lay
Athwart the chambers, and the day
Was sloping toward his western bower. 80
Then, said she, 'I am very dreary,
He will not come,' she said;
She wept, 'I am aweary, aweary,
Oh God, that I were dead!'

Recollections of the Arabian Nights

WHEN the breeze of a joyful dawn blew free
In the silken sail of infancy,
The tide of time flow'd back with me,
The forward-flowing tide of time;
And many a sheeny summer-morn, 5
Adown the Tigris I was borne,
By Bagdat's shrines of fretted gold,
High-walled gardens green and old;
True Mussulman was I and sworn,
For it was in the golden prime 10
Of good Haroun Alraschid.

Anight my shallop, rustling thro'
The low and bloomed foliage, drove
The fragrant, glistening deeps, and clove
The citron-shadows in the blue: 15
By garden porches on the brim,
The costly doors flung open wide,
Gold glittering thro' lamplight dim,
And broider'd sofas on each side:

15 *citron-shadows* presumably a reference to their colour—yellow reflections (i.e. *shadows*) in blue water

In sooth it was a goodly time,
For it was in the golden prime
Of good Haroun Alraschid.

Often, where clear-stemm'd platans guard
The outlet, did I turn away
The boat-head down a broad canal
From the main river sluiced, where all
The sloping of the moon-lit sward
Was damask-work, and deep inlay
Of braided blooms unmown, which crept
Adown to where the water slept.
A goodly place, a goodly time,
For it was in the golden prime
Of good Haroun Alraschid.

A motion from the river won
Ridged the smooth level, bearing on
My shallop thro' the star-strown calm,
Until another night in night
I enter'd, from the clearer light,
Imbower'd vaults of pillar'd palm,
Imprisoning sweets, which, as they clomb
Heavenward, were stay'd beneath the dome
Of hollow boughs.—A goodly time,
For it was in the golden prime
Of good Haroun Alraschid.

Still onward; and the clear canal
Is rounded to as clear a lake.

23 *platans* plane-trees
34 *A motion from the river won* a tide sweeping up the canal from the river

From the green rivage many a fall
Of diamond rillets musical,
Thro' little crystal arches low
Down from the central fountain's flow 50
Fall'n silver-chiming, seemed to shake
The sparkling flints beneath the prow.
  A goodly place, a goodly time,
  For it was in the golden prime
    Of good Haroun Alraschid. 55

Above thro' many a bowery turn
A walk with vary-colour'd shells
Wander'd engrain'd. On either side
All round about the fragrant marge
From fluted vase, and brazen urn 60
In order, eastern flowers large,
Some dropping low their crimson bells
Half-closed, and others studded wide
  With disks and tiars, fed the time
  With odour in the golden prime 65
    Of good Haroun Alraschid.

Far off, and where the lemon grove
In closest coverture upsprung,
The living airs of middle night
Died round the bulbul as he sung; 70
Not he: but something which possess'd
The darkness of the world, delight,

47 *rivage* shore
48 *rillets* little rills
57–8 the 'walk', or path, is 'engrain'd', or dyed, with 'vary-colour'd shells'
64 *tiars* tiaras
68 *coverture* roofing
70 *bulbul* thrush

Life, anguish, death, immortal love,
Ceasing not, mingled, unrepress'd,
Apart from place, withholding time,
But flattering the golden prime
Of good Haroun Alraschid.

Black the garden-bowers and grots
Slumber'd: the solemn palms were ranged
Above, unwoo'd of summer wind:
A sudden splendour from behind
Flush'd all the leaves with rich gold-green,
And, flowing rapidly between
Their interspaces, counterchanged
The level lake with diamond-plots
Of dark and bright. A lovely time,
For it was in the golden prime
Of good Haroun Alraschid.

Dark-blue the deep sphere overhead,
Distinct with vivid stars inlaid,
Grew darker from that under-flame:
So, leaping lightly from the boat,
With silver anchor left afloat,
In marvel whence that glory came
Upon me, as in sleep I sank
In cool soft turf upon the bank,
Entranced with that place and time,
So worthy of the golden prime
Of good Haroun Alraschid.

76 *flattering* improving
78 *grots* caves
90 *distinct* marked

Thence thro' the garden I was drawn— 100
A realm of pleasance, many a mound,
And many a shadow-chequer'd lawn
Full of the city's stilly sound,
And deep myrrh-thickets blowing round
The stately cedar, tamarisks, 105
Thick rosaries of scented thorn,
Tall orient shrubs, and obelisks
  Graven with emblems of the time,
  In honour of the golden prime
    Of good Haroun Alraschid. 110

With dazed vision unawares
From the long alley's latticed shade
Emerged, I came upon the great
Pavilion of the Caliphat.
Right to the carven cedarn doors, 115
Flung inward over spangled floors,
Broad-based flights of marble stairs
Ran up with golden balustrade,
  After the fashion of the time,
  And humour of the golden prime 120
    Of good Haroun Alraschid.

The fourscore windows all alight
As with the quintessence of flame,
A million tapers flaring bright
From twisted silvers look'd to shame 125
The hollow-vaulted dark, and stream'd
Upon the mooned domes aloof
In inmost Bagdat, till there seem'd

122 the lights in the windows of the Caliph's palace were lit only when he was in residence

Hundreds of crescents on the roof
Of night new-risen, that marvellous time 13
To celebrate the golden prime
Of good Haroun Alraschid.

Then stole I up, and trancedly
Gazed on the Persian girl alone,
Serene with argent-lidded eyes 13
Amorous, and lashes like to rays
Of darkness, and a brow of pearl
Tressed with redolent ebony,
In many a dark delicious curl,
Flowing beneath her rose-hued zone; 14
The sweetest lady of the time,
Well worthy of the golden prime
Of good Haroun Alraschid.

Six columns, three on either side,
Pure silver, underpropt a rich 14
Throne of the massive ore, from which
Down-droop'd, in many a floating fold,
Engarlanded and diaper'd
With inwrought flowers, a cloth of gold.
Thereon, his deep eye laughter-stirr'd 15
With merriment of kingly pride,
Sole star of all that place and time,
I saw him—in his golden prime,
THE GOOD HAROUN ALRASCHID.

135 *argent-lidded* silver-lidded, i.e. painted. Note the contrasting eye-lashes!
140 *zone* head-band, in this case
148 *diaper'd* here means no more than patterned

The Dying Swan

I

THE plain was grassy, wild and bare,
Wide, wild, and open to the air,
Which had built up everywhere
  An under-roof of doleful gray.
With an inner voice the river ran, 5
Adown it floated a dying swan,
    And loudly did lament.
  It was the middle of the day.
Ever the weary wind went on,
    And took the reed-tops as it went. 10

II

Some blue peaks in the distance rose,
And white against the cold-white sky,
Shone out their crowning snows.
  One willow over the river wept,
And shook the wave as the wind did sigh; 15
Above in the wind was the swallow,
    Chasing itself at its own wild will,
    And far thro' the marish green and still
    The tangled water-courses slept,
Shot over with purple, and green, and yellow. 20

III

The wild swan's death-hymn took the soul
Of that waste place with joy
Hidden in sorrow: at first to the ear
The warble was low, and full and clear;

18 *marish* see *Mariana*, l. 40

And floating about the under-sky,
Prevailing in weakness, the coronach stole
Sometimes afar, and sometimes anear:
But anon her awful jubilant voice,
With a music strange and manifold,
Flow'd forth on a carol free and bold;
As when a mighty people rejoice
With shawms, and with cymbals, and harps of gold,
And the tumult of their acclaim is roll'd
Thro' the open gates of the city afar,
To the shepherd who watcheth the evening star.
And the creeping mosses and clambering weeds,
And the willow-branches hoar and dank,
And the wavy swell of the soughing reeds,
And the wave-worn horns of the echoing bank,
And the silvery marish-flowers that throng
The desolate creeks and pools among,
Were flooded over with eddying song.

The Lady of Shalott

PART I

On either side the river lie
Long fields of barley and of rye,
That clothe the wold and meet the sky
And thro' the field the road runs by
        To many-tower'd Camelot;

25 *under-sky* the 'under-roof' of l. 4

26 *coronach* Gaelic word for a dirge or lament

32 *shawms* the shawm (mentioned in the Bible) was a mediæval instrument like an oboe

39 *wave-worn horns* the waves had hollowed the banks to the shape of curving horns

And up and down the people go,
Gazing where the lilies blow
Round an island there below,
The island of Shalott.

Willows whiten, aspens quiver, 10
Little breezes dusk and shiver
Thro' the wave that runs for ever
By the island in the river
Flowing down to Camelot.
Four gray walls, and four gray towers, 15
Overlook a space of flowers,
And the silent isle imbowers
The Lady of Shalott.

By the margin, willow-veil'd,
Slide the heavy barges trail'd 20
By slow horses; and unhail'd
The shallop flitteth silken-sail'd
Skimming down to Camelot:
But who hath seen her wave her hand?
Or at the casement seen her stand? 25
Or is she known in all the land,
The Lady of Shalott?

Only reapers, reaping early
In among the bearded barley,
Hear a song that echoes cheerly 30
From the river winding clearly,
Down to tower'd Camelot:
And by the moon the reaper weary,
Piling sheaves in uplands airy,
Listening, whispers ''Tis the fairy 35
Lady of Shalott.'

11 *dusk* the effect of a breeze on the surface of a stream is sometimes that of a dark shadow on the water

PART II

THERE she weaves by night and day
A magic web with colours gay.
She has heard a whisper say,
A curse is on her if she stay
    To look down to Camelot.
She knows not what the curse may be,
And so she weaveth steadily,
And little other care hath she,
    The Lady of Shalott.

And moving thro' a mirror clear
That hangs before her all the year,
Shadows of the world appear.
There she sees the highway near
    Winding down to Camelot:
There the river eddy whirls,
And there the surly village-churls,
And the red cloaks of market girls,
    Pass onward from Shalott.

Sometimes a troop of damsels glad,
An abbot on an ambling pad,
Sometimes a curly shepherd-lad,
Or long-hair'd page in crimson clad,
    Goes by to tower'd Camelot;
And sometimes thro' the mirror blue
The knights come riding two and two:
She hath no loyal knight and true,
    The Lady of Shalott.

56 *pad* 'an easy-paced horse' (O.E.D.)

But in her web she still delights
To weave the mirror's magic sights, 65
For often thro' the silent nights
A funeral, with plumes and lights
And music, went to Camelot:
Or when the moon was overhead,
Came two young lovers lately wed; 70
'I am half sick of shadows,' said
The Lady of Shalott.

PART III

A BOW-SHOT from her bower-eaves,
He rode between the barley-sheaves,
The sun came dazzling thro' the leaves, 75
And flamed upon the brazen greaves
Of bold Sir Lancelot.
A red-cross knight for ever kneel'd
To a lady in his shield,
That sparkled on the yellow field, 80
Beside remote Shalott.

The gemmy bridle glitter'd free,
Like to some branch of stars we see
Hung in the golden Galaxy.
The bridle bells rang merrily 85
As he rode down to Camelot:
And from his blazon'd baldric slung
A mighty silver bugle hung,
And as he rode his armour rung,
Beside remote Shalott. 90

76 *greaves* armour which covered the leg from knee to ankle
84 *Galaxy* the Milky Way
87 *blazon'd baldric* a belt slung from one shoulder across the chest, adorned with a heraldic device (emblazoned)

All in the blue unclouded weather
Thick-jewell'd shone the saddle-leather,
The helmet and the helmet-feather
Burn'd like one burning flame together,
As he rode down to Camelot. 9
As often thro' the purple night,
Below the starry clusters bright,
Some bearded meteor, trailing light,
Moves over still Shalott.

His broad clear brow in sunlight glow'd; 10
On burnish'd hooves his war-horse trode;
From underneath his helmet flow'd
His coal-black curls as on he rode,
As he rode down to Camelot.
From the bank and from the river 10
He flash'd into the crystal mirror,
'Tirra lirra,' by the river
Sang Sir Lancelot.

She left the web, she left the loom,
She made three paces thro' the room, 11
She saw the water-lily bloom,
She saw the helmet and the plume,
She look'd down to Camelot.
Out flew the web and floated wide;
The mirror crack'd from side to side; 11
'The curse is come upon me,' cried
The Lady of Shalott.

96–8 note here, as in l. 84, Tennyson's early interest in the stars

PART IV

In the stormy east-wind straining,
The pale yellow woods were waning,
The broad stream in his banks complaining, 120
Heavily the low sky raining
        Over tower'd Camelot;
Down she came and found a boat
Beneath a willow left afloat,
And round about the prow she wrote 125
        The Lady of Shalott.

And down the river's dim expanse
Like some bold seër in a trance,
Seeing all his own mischance—
With a glassy countenance 130
        Did she look to Camelot.
And at the closing of the day
She loosed the chain, and down she lay;
The broad stream bore her far away,
        The Lady of Shalott. 135

Lying, robed in snowy white
That loosely flew to left and right—
The leaves upon her falling light—
Thro' the noises of the night
        She floated down to Camelot: 140
And as the boat-head wound along
The willowy hills and fields among,
They heard her singing her last song,
        The Lady of Shalott.

Heard a carol, mournful, holy, 145
Chanted loudly, chanted lowly,
Till her blood was frozen slowly,

And her eyes were darken'd wholly,
Turn'd to tower'd Camelot.
For ere she reach'd upon the tide 150
The first house by the water-side,
Singing in her song she died,
The Lady of Shalott.

Under tower and balcony,
By garden-wall and gallery, 155
A gleaming shape she floated by,
Dead-pale between the houses high,
Silent into Camelot.
Out upon the wharfs they came,
Knight and burgher, lord and dame, 160
And round the prow they read her name,
The Lady of Shalott.

Who is this? and what is here?
And in the lighted palace near
Died the sound of royal cheer; 16
And they cross'd themselves for fear,
All the knights at Camelot:
But Lancelot mused a little space;
He said, 'She has a lovely face;
God in his mercy lend her grace, 17
The Lady of Shalott.'

Œnone

THERE lies a vale in Ida, lovelier
Than all the valleys of Ionian hills.
The swimming vapour slopes athwart the glen,
Puts forth an arm, and creeps from pine to pine,

1 *Ida* for place-names see *Notes*

And loiters, slowly drawn. On either hand 5
The lawns and meadow-ledges midway down
Hang rich in flowers, and far below them roars
The long brook falling thro' the clov'n ravine
In cataract after cataract to the sea.
Behind the valley topmost Gargarus 10
Stands up and takes the morning: but in front
The gorges, opening wide apart, reveal
Troas and Ilion's column'd citadel,
The crown of Troas.

Hither came at noon
Mournful Œnone, wandering forlorn 15
Of Paris, once her playmate on the hills.
Her cheek had lost the rose, and round her neck
Floated her hair or seem'd to float in rest.
She, leaning on a fragment twined with vine,
Sang to the stillness, till the mountain-shade 20
Sloped downward to her seat from the upper cliff.

'O mother Ida, many-fountain'd Ida,
Dear mother Ida, harken ere I die.
For now the noonday quiet holds the hill:
The grasshopper is silent in the grass: 25
The lizard, with his shadow on the stone,
Rests like a shadow, and the winds are dead.
The purple flower droops: the golden bee
Is lily-cradled: I alone awake.
My eyes are full of tears, my heart of love, 30
My heart is breaking, and my eyes are dim,
And I am all aweary of my life.

15–16 *forlorn of Paris* deserted by Paris; but *forlorn* carries its own sense of dejection

'O mother Ida, many-fountain'd Ida,
Dear mother Ida, harken ere I die.
Hear me, O Earth, hear me, O Hills, O Caves 35
That house the cold crown'd snake! O mountain brooks,
I am the daughter of a River-God,
Hear me, for I will speak, and build up all
My sorrow with my song, as yonder walls
Rose slowly to a music slowly breathed, 40
A cloud that gather'd shape: for it may be
That, while I speak of it, a little while
My heart may wander from its deeper woe.

'O mother Ida, many-fountain'd Ida,
Dear mother Ida, harken ere I die. 45
I waited underneath the dawning hills,
Aloft the mountain lawn was dewy-dark,
And dewy-dark aloft the mountain pine:
Beautiful Paris, evil-hearted Paris,
Leading a jet-black goat white-horn'd, white-hooved, 50
Came up from reedy Simois all alone.

'O mother Ida, harken ere I die.
Far-off the torrent call'd me from the cleft:
Far up the solitary morning smote
The streaks of virgin snow. With down-dropt eyes 55
I sat alone: white-breasted like a star
Fronting the dawn he moved; a leopard skin
Droop'd from his shoulder, but his sunny hair
Cluster'd about his temples like a God's:
And his cheek brighten'd as the foam-bow brightens 60

39–40 Troy was said by one legend to have been miraculously built. As Apollo played his lyre the stones moved into place of themselves
60 *foam-bow* rainbow of foam, or spray, above a waterfall

When the wind blows the foam, and all my heart
Went forth to embrace him coming ere he came.

'Dear mother Ida, harken ere I die.
He smiled, and opening out his milk-white palm
Disclosed a fruit of pure Hesperian gold 65
That smelt ambrosially, and while I look'd
And listen'd, the full-flowing river of speech
Came down upon my heart.
' "My own Œnone,
Beautiful-brow'd Œnone, my own soul,
Behold this fruit, whose gleaming rind ingrav'n 70
'For the most fair,' would seem to award it thine,
As lovelier than whatever Oread haunt
The knolls of Ida, loveliest in all grace
Of movement, and the charm of married brows."

'Dear mother Ida, harken ere I die. 75
He prest the blossom of his lips to mine,
And added "This was cast upon the board,
When all the full-faced presence of the Gods
Ranged in the halls of Peleus; whereupon
Rose feud, with question unto whom 'twere due: 80
But light-foot Iris brought it yester-eve,
Delivering, that to me, by common voice
Elected umpire, Herè comes to-day,

62 *him coming* him as he came; a classical touch
72 *haunt* printed thus in all editions. Since 'Oread' (mountain nymph) is singular, *haunts* would seem more correct
74 what are 'married brows'? Would they be considered especially 'charming' today?
78 *full-faced* presumably the Gods were all sitting round 'the board' (l. 77) facing each other
79 *Peleus* for the story see *Notes*
82 *Delivering* announcing

Pallas and Aphroditè, claiming each
This meed of fairest. Thou, within the cave 85
Behind yon whispering tuft of oldest pine,
Mayst well behold them unbeheld, unheard
Hear all, and see thy Paris judge of Gods."

'Dear mother Ida, harken ere I die.
It was the deep midnoon: one silvery cloud 90
Had lost his way between the piney sides
Of this long glen. Then to the bower they came,
Naked they came to that smooth-swarded bower,
And at their feet the crocus brake like fire,
Violet, amaracus, and asphodel, 95
Lotos and lilies: and a wind arose,
And overhead the wandering ivy and vine,
This way and that, in many a wild festoon
Ran riot, garlanding the gnarled boughs
With bunch and berry and flower thro' and thro'. 100

'O mother Ida, harken ere I die.
On the tree-tops a crested peacock lit,
And o'er him flow'd a golden cloud, and lean'd
Upon him, slowly dropping fragrant dew.
Then first I heard the voice of her, to whom 105
Coming thro' Heaven, like a light that grows
Larger and clearer, with one mind the Gods
Rise up for reverence. She to Paris made
Proffer of royal power, ample rule
Unquestion'd, overflowing revenue 110

94 *brake like fire* each petal, when the flower opens, is shaped like a flame. Some crocuses, also, would be flame-coloured
95 *amaracus* marjoram *asphodel* a kind of lily
102 *peacock* a frequent attendant on Hera

Wherewith to embellish state, "from many a vale
And river-sunder'd champaign clothed with corn,
Or labour'd mine undrainable of ore.
Honour," she said, "and homage, tax and toll,
From many an inland town and haven large, 115
Mast-throng'd beneath her shadowing citadel
In glassy bays among her tallest towers."

'O mother Ida, harken ere I die.
Still she spake on and still she spake of power,
"Which in all action is the end of all; 120
Power fitted to the season; wisdom-bred
And throned of wisdom—from all neighbour crowns
Alliance and allegiance, till thy hand
Fail from the sceptre-staff. Such boon from me,
From me, Heaven's Queen, Paris, to thee king-born, 125
A shepherd all thy life but yet king-born,
Should come most welcome, seeing men, in power
Only, are likest gods, who have attain'd
Rest in a happy place and quiet seats
Above the thunder, with undying bliss 130
In knowledge of their own supremacy."

'Dear mother Ida, harken ere I die.
She ceased, and Paris held the costly fruit
Out at arm's-length, so much the thought of power
Flatter'd his spirit; but Pallas where she stood 135
Somewhat apart, her clear and bared limbs
O'erthwarted with the brazen-headed spear
Upon her pearly shoulder leaning cold,

111 *to embellish state* to keep up, and beautify, royal position
112 *river-sunder'd champaign* fields intersected (and irrigated) by rivers
137 *O'erthwarted* crossed

The while, above, her full and earnest eye
Over her snow-cold breast and angry cheek 140
Kept watch, waiting decision, made reply.

'" Self-reverence, self-knowledge, self-control,
These three alone lead life to sovereign power.
Yet not for power (power of herself
Would come uncall'd for) but to live by law, 145
Acting the law we live by without fear;
And, because right is right, to follow right
Were wisdom in the scorn of consequence."

'Dear mother Ida, harken ere I die.
Again she said: "I woo thee not with gifts. 150
Sequel of guerdon could not alter me
To fairer. Judge thou me by what I am,
So shalt thou find me fairest.

Yet, indeed,

If gazing on divinity disrobed
Thy mortal eyes are frail to judge of fair, 155
Unbias'd by self-profit, oh! rest thee sure
That I shall love thee well and cleave to thee,
So that my vigour, wedded to thy blood,
Shall strike within thy pulses, like a God's,
To push thee forward thro' a life of shocks, 160
Dangers, and deeds, until endurance grow

140 why '*angry* cheek'?

151 *Sequel of guerdon* the promise of a reward (*guerdon*) to follow (*sequel*)

154–6 if, being only human, your judgement is upset by the sight of a naked goddess, and you are unable to judge beauty impartially (i.e., without any question of 'self-profit')

Sinew'd with action, and the full-grown will,
Circled thro' all experiences, pure law,
Commeasure perfect freedom."

'Here she ceas'd,
And Paris ponder'd, and I cried, "O Paris, 165
Give it to Pallas!" but he heard me not,
Or hearing would not hear me, woe is me!

'O mother Ida, many fountain'd Ida,
Dear mother Ida, harken ere I die.
Idalian Aphroditè beautiful, 170
Fresh as the foam, new bathed in Paphian wells,
With rosy slender fingers backward drew
From her warm brows and bosom her deep hair
Ambrosial, golden round her lucid throat
And shoulder: from the violets her light foot 175
Shone rosy-white, and o'er her rounded form
Between the shadows of the vine-bunches
Floated the glowing sunlights, as she moved.

'Dear mother Ida, harken ere I die.
She with a subtle smile in her mild eyes, 180
The herald of her triumph, drawing nigh
Half-whisper'd in his ear, "I promise thee
The fairest and most loving wife in Greece,"
She spoke and laugh'd: I shut my sight for fear:
But when I look'd, Paris had raised his arm, 185
And I beheld great Herè's angry eyes,

162 *Sinew'd with action* strengthened by exercise

162–4 and the will, fully grown, after 'circling' through 'all experience', becomes identified with the highest ('pure') law, which is the same as perfect freedom. The meaning, as befits Pallas, is lofty and obscure

174 *ambrosial* a favourite word with Tennyson. Ambrosia was the food of the gods (what was their drink?) so *ambrosial* can mean rich, beautiful, fragrant, etc.

As she withdrew into the golden cloud,
And I was left alone within the bower;
And from that time to this I am alone,
And I shall be alone until I die. 190

'Yet, mother Ida, harken ere I die.
Fairest—why fairest wife? am I not fair?
My love hath told me so a thousand times.
Methinks I must be fair, for yesterday,
When I past by, a wild and wanton pard, 195
Eyed like the evening star, with playful tail
Crouch'd fawning in the weed. Most loving is she?
Ah me, my mountain shepherd, that my arms
Were wound about thee, and my hot lips prest
Close, close to thine in that quick-falling dew 200
Of fruitful kisses, thick as Autumn rains
Flash in the pools of whirling Simois.

'O mother, hear me yet before I die.
They came, they cut away my tallest pines,
My tall dark pines, that plumed the craggy ledge 205
High over the blue gorge, and all between
The snowy peak and snow-white cataract
Foster'd the callow eaglet—from beneath
Whose thick mysterious boughs in the dark morn
The panther's roar came muffled, while I sat 210
Low in the valley. Never, never more
Shall lone Œnone see the morning mist
Sweep thro' them; never see them overlaid
With narrow moon-lit slips of silver cloud,
Between the loud stream and the trembling stars. 215

195 *pard* leopard. Beauty, according to the classical poets, had the power to tame leopards and some other wild animals
204 the pine-trees were cut down to make ships for Paris's fleet
208 *callow* unfledged

'O mother, hear me yet before I die.
I wish that somewhere in the ruin'd folds,
Among the fragments tumbled from the glens,
Or the dry thickets, I could meet with her
The Abominable, that uninvited came 220
Into the fair Peleïan banquet-hall,
And cast the golden fruit upon the board,
And bred this change; that I might speak my mind,
And tell her to her face how much I hate
Her presence, hated both of Gods and men. 225

'O mother, hear me yet before I die.
Hath he not sworn his love a thousand times,
In this green valley, under this green hill,
Ev'n on this hand, and sitting on this stone?
Seal'd it with kisses? water'd it with tears? 230
O happy tears, and how unlike to these!
O happy Heaven, how canst thou see my face?
O happy earth, how canst thou bear my weight?
O death, death, death, thou ever-floating cloud,
There are enough unhappy on this earth, 235
Pass by the happy souls, that love to live;
I pray thee, pass before my light of life,
And shadow all my soul, that I may die.
Thou weighest heavy on the heart within,
Weigh heavy on my eyelids: let me die. 240

'O mother, hear me yet before I die.
I will not die alone, for fiery thoughts
Do shape themselves within me, more and more,
Whereof I catch the issue, as I hear

220 *The Abominable* Eris, goddess of Strife, who started it all
236, 237 note the difference between 'pass by' and 'pass before'
243–4, 247 a foreshadowing of the end of Œnone's story (see *Notes*)

Dead sounds at night come from the inmost hills, 245
Like footsteps upon wool. I dimly see
My far-off doubtful purpose, as a mother
Conjectures of the features of her child
Ere it is born: her child!—a shudder comes
Across me: never child be born of me, 250
Unblest, to vex me with his father's eyes!

'O mother, hear me yet before I die.
Hear me, O earth. I will not die alone,
Lest their shrill happy laughter come to me
Walking the cold and starless road of Death 255
Uncomforted, leaving my ancient love
With the Greek woman. I will rise and go
Down into Troy, and ere the stars come forth
Talk with the wild Cassandra, for she says
A fire dances before her, and a sound 260
Rings ever in her ears of armed men.
What this may be I know not, but I know
That, wheresoe'er I am by night and day,
All earth and air seem only burning fire.'

The Lotos-Eaters

'COURAGE!' he said, and pointed toward the land,
'This mounting wave will roll us shoreward soon.'
In the afternoon they came unto a land
In which it seemed always afternoon.
All round the coast the languid air did swoon, 5
Breathing like one that hath a weary dream.
Full-faced above the valley stood the moon;

1 *he* Ulysses

And like a downward smoke, the slender stream
Along the cliff to fall and pause and fall did seem.
A land of streams! some, like a downward smoke, 10
Slow-dropping veils of thinnest lawn, did go;
And some thro' wavering lights and shadows broke,
Rolling a slumbrous sheet of foam below.
They saw the gleaming river seaward flow
From the inner land: far off, three mountain-tops, 15
Three silent pinnacles of aged snow,
Stood sunset-flush'd: and, dew'd with showery drops,
Up-clomb the shadowy pine above the woven copse.

The charmed sunset linger'd low adown
In the red West: thro' mountain clefts the dale 20
Was seen far inland, and the yellow down
Border'd with palm, and many a winding vale
And meadow, set with slender galingale;
A land where all things always seem'd the same!
And round about the keel with faces pale, 25
Dark faces pale against that rosy flame,
The mild-eyed melancholy Lotos-eaters came.

Branches they bore of that enchanted stem,
Laden with flower and fruit, whereof they gave
To each, but whoso did receive of them, 30
And taste, to him the gushing of the wave
Far far away did seem to mourn and rave

11 *lawn* fine linen (from Laon, in France)

18 *Up-clomb* climbed up. A Tennysonian word. Note the extra foot in this line to add to the effect of languor (see *Notes*)

23 *galingale* a plant of the marshes in Western Europe. In the East, an aromatic plant with a root used for flavouring. Tennyson subtly suggests both meanings

26 *that rosy flame* what rosy flame?

On alien shores; and if his fellow spake,
His voice was thin, as voices from the grave;
And deep-asleep he seem'd, yet all awake, 35
And music in his ears his beating heart did make.

They sat them down upon the yellow sand,
Between the sun and moon upon the shore;
And sweet it was to dream of Fatherland,
Of child, and wife, and slave; but evermore 40
Most weary seem'd the sea, weary the oar,
Weary the wandering fields of barren foam.
Then some one said, 'We will return no more;'
And all at once they sang, 'Our island home
Is far beyond the wave; we will no longer roam.' 45

Choric Song

I

THERE is sweet music here that softer falls
Than petals from blown roses on the grass,
Or night-dews on still waters between walls
Of shadowy granite, in a gleaming pass;
Music that gentlier on the spirit lies, 50
Than tir'd eyelids upon tir'd eyes;
Music that brings sweet sleep down from the blissful
skies.
Here are cool mosses deep,
And thro' the moss the ivies creep,
And in the stream the long-leaved flowers weep, 55
And from the craggy ledge the poppy hangs in sleep.

44 *all at once* all together, not suddenly

Choric Song song sung in chorus

II

Why are we weigh'd upon with heaviness,
And utterly consumed with sharp distress,
While all things else have rest from weariness?
All things have rest: why should we toil alone, 60
We only toil, who are the first of things,
And make perpetual moan,
Still from one sorrow to another thrown:
Nor ever fold our wings,
And cease from wanderings, 65
Nor steep our brows in slumber's holy balm;
Nor harken what the inner spirit sings,
'There is no joy but calm!'
Why should we only toil, the roof and crown of
things?

III

Lo! in the middle of the wood, 70
The folded leaf is woo'd from out the bud
With winds upon the branch, and there
Grows green and broad, and takes no care,
Sun-steep'd at noon, and in the moon
Nightly dew-fed; and turning yellow 75
Falls, and floats adown the air.
Lo! sweeten'd with the summer light,
The full-juiced apple, waxing over-mellow,
Drops in a silent autumn night.
All its allotted length of days, 80
The flower ripens in its place,
Ripens and fades, and falls, and hath no toil,
Fast-rooted in the fruitful soil.

61 *the first of things* masters of creation, i.e. human beings

IV

Hateful is the dark-blue sky,
Vaulted o'er the dark-blue sea. 85
Death is the end of life; ah, why
Should life all labour be?
Let us alone. Time driveth onward fast,
And in a little while our lips are dumb.
Let us alone. What is it that will last? 90
All things are taken from us, and become
Portions and parcels of the dreadful Past.
Let us alone. What pleasure can we have
To war with evil? Is there any peace
In ever climbing up the climbing wave? 95
All things have rest, and ripen toward the grave
In silence; ripen, fall and cease:
Give us long rest or death, dark death, or dreamful
ease.

V

How sweet it were, hearing the downward stream, 100
With half-shut eyes ever to seem
Falling asleep in a half-dream!
To dream and dream, like yonder amber light,
Which will not leave the myrrh-bush on the height;
To hear each other's whisper'd speech;
Eating the Lotos day by day, 105
To watch the crisping ripples on the beach,
And tender curving lines of creamy spray;
To lend our hearts and spirits wholly
To the influence of mild-minded melancholy;
To muse and brood and live again in memory, 110
With those old faces of our infancy
Heap'd over with a mound of grass,
Two handfuls of white dust, shut in an urn of brass!

VI

Dear is the memory of our wedded lives,
And dear the last embraces of our wives 115
And their warm tears: but all hath suffer'd change:
For surely now our household hearths are cold:
Our sons inherit us: our looks are strange:
And we should come like ghosts to trouble joy.
Or else the island princes over-bold 120
Have eat our substance, and the minstrel sings
Before them of the ten years' war in Troy,
And our great deeds, as half-forgotten things.
Is there confusion in the little isle?
Let what is broken so remain. 125
The Gods are hard to reconcile:
'Tis hard to settle order once again.
There *is* confusion worse than death,
Trouble on trouble, pain on pain,
Long labour unto aged breath, 130
Sore task to hearts worn out by many wars
And eyes grown dim with gazing on the pilot-stars.

VII

But, propt on beds of amaranth and moly,
How sweet (while warm airs lull us, blowing lowly)

120 *the island princes* the mariners have been away at the siege of Troy for ten years. In their absence their wives may have been wooed by other suitors as, we are told by Homer, Ulysses' wife, Penelope, had been pestered by 'the island princes'

121 *Have eat our substance* subtly suggests the suitors feasting themselves in their houses while the husbands are away

130 *unto aged breath* until we are old

132 *pilot-stars* by which the helmsman steered at night

133 *amaranth* the imaginary flower that never fades. (But there *is* a genuine plant of the same name, with coloured leaves)

moly another fabulous plant, used as a charm against sorcerers

With half-dropt eyelid still, 13
Beneath a heaven dark and holy,
To watch the long bright river drawing slowly
His waters from the purple hill—
To hear the dewy echoes calling
From cave to cave thro' the thick-twined vine— 14
To watch the emerald-colour'd water falling
Thro' many a wov'n acanthus-wreath divine!
Only to hear and see the far-off sparkling brine,
Only to hear were sweet, stretch'd out beneath the pine.

VIII

The Lotos blooms below the barren peak: 14
The Lotos blows by every winding creek:
All day the wind breathes low with mellower tone:
Thro' every hollow cave and alley lone
Round and round the spicy downs the yellow Lotos-dust is blown.
We have had enough of action, and of motion we, 15
Roll'd to starboard, roll'd to larboard, when the surge was seething free,
Where the wallowing monster spouted his foam-fountains in the sea.
Let us swear an oath, and keep it with an equal mind,
In the hollow Lotos-land to live and lie reclined
On the hills like Gods together, careless of mankind. 15
For they lie beside their nectar, and the bolts are hurl'd

142 *acanthus-wreath* intertwined acanthus-plants. This is a graceful plant, with a leaf which provided a popular subject in Greek sculpture and architecture

153 *with an equal mind* without wavering

154 *hollow* full of caves

Far below them in the valleys, and the clouds are lightly
curl'd
Round their golden houses, girdled with the gleaming
world:
Where they smile in secret, looking over wasted
lands,
Blight and famine, plague and earthquake, roaring
deeps and fiery sands, 160
Clanging fights, and flaming towns, and sinking ships,
and praying hands.
But they smile, they find a music centred in a doleful
song
Steaming up, a lamentation and an ancient tale of
wrong,
Like a tale of little meaning tho' the words are
strong;
Chanted from an ill-used race of men that cleave the
soil, 165
Sow the seed, and reap the harvest with enduring toil,
Storing yearly little dues of wheat, and wine and oil;
Till they perish and they suffer—some, 'tis whisper'd
—down in hell
Suffer endless anguish, others in Elysian valleys dwell,
Resting weary limbs at last on beds of asphodel. 170
Surely, surely, slumber is more sweet than toil, the
shore
Than labour in the deep mid-ocean, wind and wave
and oar;
Oh rest ye, brother mariners, we will not wander
more.

167 *little dues* presumably the small quantities required for 'rents' or tithes. But in that case why store them?

Of Old Sat Freedom

OF old sat Freedom on the heights,
  The thunders breaking at her feet:
Above her shook the starry lights:
  She heard the torrents meet.

There in her place she did rejoice,
  Self-gather'd in her prophet-mind,
But fragments of her mighty voice
  Came rolling on the wind.

Then stept she down thro' town and field
  To mingle with the human race,
And part by part to men reveal'd
  The fullness of her face—

Grave mother of majestic works,
  From her isle-altar gazing down,
Who, God-like, grasps the triple forks,
  And, King-like, wears the crown:

Her open eyes desire the truth.
  The wisdom of a thousand years
Is in them. May perpetual youth
  Keep dry their light from tears;

6 a vague and poetic way of saying that Freedom sat alone ('self-gather'd'), with her thoughts ('in her prophet-mind'). 'Prophet' is here used with its meaning of wise man rather than foreteller of the future

7–8 men heard her voice—i.e., learned something of what Freedom means—by occasional revelations

14 Tennyson suggests that Freedom has set her throne in Britain ('her *isle*-altar'). She 'grasps the triple forks'—as Britannia does—to imply mastery of the seas. (Neptune grasped a trident and was god of the seas)

That her fair form may stand and shine,
  Make bright our days and light our dreams,
Turning to scorn with lips divine
  The falsehood of extremes!

You Ask Me Why

You ask me, why, tho' ill at ease,
  Within this region I subsist,
  Whose spirits falter in the mist,
And languish for the purple seas.

It is the land that freemen till, 5
  That sober-suited Freedom chose,
  The land, where girt with friends or foes
A man may speak the thing he will;

A land of settled government,
  A land of just and old renown, 10
  Where Freedom slowly broadens down
From precedent to precedent:

Where faction seldom gathers head,
  But by degrees to fullness wrought,
  The strength of some diffusive thought 15
Hath time and space to work and spread.

3 *whose* 'I . . . whose spirits falter . . .'

11–12 by Freedom, Tennyson means rather the laws which bring or create freedom. The law of England is to a great extent like the British Constitution, in that it is created by precedents rather than laid down from the first in black and white

13–16 'faction', i.e., party strife or dissension, does not come violently to a sudden 'head' but grows slowly. A new political idea ('some diffusive thought') has space and freedom to grow and spread peacefully

Should banded unions persecute
Opinion, and induce a time
When single thought is civil crime,
And individual freedom mute;

Tho' Power should make from land to land
The name of Britain trebly great—
Tho' every channel of the State
Should fill and choke with golden sand—

Yet waft me from the harbour-mouth,
Wild wind! I seek a warmer sky,
And I will see before I die
The palms and temples of the South.

Morte D'Arthur

So all day long the noise of battle roll'd
Among the mountains by the winter sea;
Until King Arthur's table, man by man,
Had fallen in Lyonnesse about their Lord,
King Arthur: then, because his wound was deep,
The bold Sir Bedivere uplifted him,
Sir Bedivere, the last of all his knights,
And bore him to a chapel nigh the field,
A broken chancel with a broken cross,

19 *single* individual; the thought of a minority; singular

4 *Lyonnesse* see *Notes*

9–12 probably symbolic. The ruined chancel and cross suggest the ruin of King Arthur's high purpose in life; the narrow land between the ocean and the lake is the 'great divide', with Life on one side, Death on the other

That stood on a dark strait of barren land. 10
On one side lay the Ocean, and on one
Lay a great water, and the moon was full.
Then spake King Arthur to Sir Bedivere:
'The sequel of to-day unsolders all
The goodliest fellowship of famous knights 15
Whereof this world holds record. Such a sleep
They sleep—the men I loved. I think that we
Shall never more, at any future time,
Delight our souls with talk of knightly deeds,
Walking about the gardens and the halls 20
Of Camelot, as in the days that were.
I perish by this people which I made,—
Tho' Merlin sware that I should come again
To rule once more—but let what will be, be,
I am so deeply smitten thro' the helm 25
That without help I cannot last till morn.
Thou therefore take my brand Excalibur,
Which was my pride: for thou rememberest how
In those old days, one summer noon, an arm
Rose up from out the bosom of the lake, 30
Clothed in white samite, mystic, wonderful,
Holding the sword—and how I row'd across
And took it, and have worn it, like a king:
And, wheresoever I am sung or told
In aftertime, this also shall be known: 35
But now delay not: take Excalibur,

14 *unsolders* the word has a modern look but *solder* (Lat. *solidare*, to make solid) is a 16th-century word

27 *Excalibur* Malory says the name meant cut-steel but the derivation is obscure. Another name for it was Caliburn. See the description in *The Coming of Arthur*

31 *samite* a rich silk embroidered or interwoven with gold thread

And fling him far into the middle mere:
Watch what thou seëst, and lightly bring me word.'
    To him replied the bold Sir Bedivere:
'It is not meet, Sir King, to leave thee thus,
Aidless, alone, and smitten thro' the helm.
A little thing may harm a wounded man.
Yet I thy hest will all perform at full,
Watch what I see, and lightly bring thee word.'
    So saying, from the ruin'd shrine he stept
And in the moon athwart the place of tombs,
Where lay the mighty bones of ancient men,
Old knights, and over them the sea-wind sang
Shrill, chill, with flakes of foam. He, stepping down
By zig-zag paths, and juts of pointed rock,
Came on the shining levels of the lake.
    There drew he forth the brand Excalibur,
And o'er him, drawing it, the winter moon,
Brightening the skirts of a long cloud, ran forth
And sparkled keen with frost against the hilt:
For all the haft twinkled with diamond sparks,
Myriads of topaz-lights, and jacinth-work
Of subtlest jewellery. He gazed so long
That both his eyes were dazzled, as he stood,
This way and that dividing the swift mind,
In act to throw: but at the last it seem'd
Better to leave Excalibur conceal'd
There in the many-knotted waterflags,
That whistled stiff and dry about the marge.

37 *the middle mere* the middle of the lake. A Latin construction. (Cf. *in medias res* in the middle of things)
53 *o'er him, drawing it* another Latin construction
57 *jacinth* 'among the ancients a gem of blue colour, probably sapphire.' (O.E.D.) The word is the same as *hyacinth*
60 this line is a straight translation of a line in the *Aeneid*

So strode he back slow to the wounded King. 65
Then spake King Arthur to Sir Bedivere:
'Hast thou perform'd my mission which I gave?
What is it thou hast seen? or what hast heard?'
And answer made the bold Sir Bedivere:
'I heard the ripple washing in the reeds, 70
And the wild water lapping on the crag.'
To whom replied King Arthur, faint and pale:
'Thou hast betray'd thy nature and thy name,
Not rendering true answer, as beseem'd
Thy fëalty, nor like a noble knight: 75
For surer sign had follow'd, either hand,
Or voice, or else a motion of the mere.
This is a shameful thing for men to lie.
Yet now, I charge thee, quickly go again
As thou art lief and dear, and do the thing 80
I bad thee, watch, and lightly bring me word.'
Then went Sir Bedivere the second time
Across the ridge, and paced beside the mere,
Counting the dewy pebbles, fix'd in thought;
But when he saw the wonder of the hilt, 85
How curiously and strangely chased, he smote
His palms together, and he cried aloud,
'And if indeed I cast the brand away,
Surely a precious thing, one worthy note,
Should thus be lost for ever from the earth, 90
Which might have pleased the eyes of many men.
What good should follow this, if this were done?
What harm, undone? deep harm to disobey,
Seeing obedience is the bond of rule.

75 *fëalty* literally the allegiance owed by a vassal to his feudal lord
80 *lief* beloved
84 why should Sir Bedivere count the pebbles?
93 *What harm, undone?* if it were not done

Were it well to obey then, if a king demand
An act unprofitable, against himself?
The King is sick, and knows not what he does.
What record, or what relic of my lord
Should be to aftertime, but empty breath
And rumours of a doubt? but were this kept,
Stored in some treasure-house of mighty kings,
Some one might show it at a joust of arms,
Saying, "King Arthur's sword, Excalibur,
Wrought by the lonely maiden of the Lake.
Nine years she wrought it, sitting in the deeps
Upon the hidden bases of the hills."
So might some old man speak in the aftertime
To all the people, winning reverence.
But now much honour and much fame were lost.'
    So spake he, clouded with his own conceit,
And hid Excalibur the second time,
And so strode back slow to the wounded King.
    Then spoke King Arthur, breathing heavily:
'What is it thou hast seen? or what hast heard?'
    And answer made the bold Sir Bedivere:
'I heard the water lapping on the crag,
And the long ripple washing in the reeds.'
    To whom replied King Arthur, much in wrath:
'Ah, miserable and unkind, untrue,
Unknightly, traitor-hearted! Woe is me!
Authority forgets a dying king,
Laid widow'd of the power in his eye
That bow'd the will. I see thee what thou art,
For thou, the latest-left of all my knights,

110 *clouded . . . conceit* deceived by his own argument
conceit idea

In whom should meet the offices of all, 125
Thou wouldst betray me for the precious hilt;
Either from lust of gold, or like a girl
Valuing the giddy pleasure of the eyes.
Yet, for a man may fail in duty twice,
And the third time may prosper, get thee hence: 130
But, if thou spare to fling Excalibur,
I will arise and slay thee with my hands.'
  Then quickly rose Sir Bedivere, and ran,
And, leaping down the ridges lightly, plunged
Among the bulrush-beds, and clutch'd the sword, 135
And strongly wheel'd and threw it. The great brand
Made lightnings in the splendour of the moon,
And flashing round and round, and whirl'd in an arch,
Shot like a streamer of the northern morn,
Seen where the moving isles of winter shock 140
By night, with noises of the northern sea.
So flash'd and fell the brand Excalibur:
But ere he dipt the surface, rose an arm
Clothed in white samite, mystic, wonderful,
And caught him by the hilt, and brandish'd him 145
Three times, and drew him under in the mere.
And lightly went the other to the King.
  Then spoke King Arthur, drawing thicker breath:
'Now see I by thine eyes that this is done.
Speak out: what is it thou hast heard, or seen?' 150
  And answer made the bold Sir Bedivere:
'Sir King, I closed mine eyelids, lest the gems
Should blind my purpose, for I never saw,

125 in whom the duties (offices) of all the knights should now reside (as the others are all gone)

139 *a streamer . . .* Aurora Borealis

140 *moving isles of winter* icebergs

145 *brandish'd* almost a technical term for waving a sword

Nor shall see, here or elsewhere, till I die,
Not tho' I live three lives of mortal men,
So great a miracle as yonder hilt.
Then with both hands I flung him, wheeling him;
But when I look'd again, behold an arm,
Clothed in white samite, mystic, wonderful,
That caught him by the hilt, and brandish'd him
Three times, and drew him under in the mere.'
    And answer made King Arthur, breathing hard:
'My end draws nigh; 'tis time that I were gone.
Make broad thy shoulders to receive my weight,
And bear me to the margin; yet I fear
My wound hath taken cold, and I shall die.'
    So saying, from the pavement he half rose,
Slowly, with pain, reclining on his arm,
And looking wistfully with wide blue eyes
As in a picture. Him Sir Bedivere
Remorsefully regarded thro' his tears,
And would have spoken, but he found not words,
Then took with care, and kneeling on one knee,
O'er both his shoulders drew the languid hands,
And rising bore him thro' the place of tombs.
    But, as he walk'd, King Arthur panted hard,
Like one that feels a nightmare on his bed
When all the house is mute. So sigh'd the King,
Muttering and murmuring at his ear, 'Quick, quick!
I fear it is too late, and I shall die.'
But the other swiftly strode from ridge to ridge,
Clothed with his breath, and looking, as he walk'd,

165 *margin* the shore
167 *pavement* the stone floor (of the chapel)
170 *As in a picture* with the lifeless, unmoving eyes of a portrait
182 *clothed with his breath* what picture does this phrase conjure up?

Larger than human on the frozen hills.
He heard the deep behind him, and a cry
Before. His own thought drove him, like a goad. 185
Dry clash'd his harness in the icy caves
And barren chasms, and all to left and right
The bare black cliff clang'd round him, as he based
His feet on juts of slippery crag that rang
Sharp-smitten with the dint of armed heels— 190
And on a sudden, lo! the level lake,
And the long glories of the winter moon.
Then saw they how there hove a dusky barge,
Dark as a funeral scarf from stem to stern,
Beneath them; and descending they were ware 195
That all the decks were dense with stately forms
Black-stoled, black-hooded, like a dream—by these
Three Queens with crowns of gold—and from them rose
A cry that shiver'd to the tingling stars,
And, as it were one voice an agony 200

183 *larger than human* figures often seem larger than they are when seen through mist

186–92 this is one of the most famous examples of onomatopœia in the language (see *Introduction*, p. 24)

186 *harness* armour. The use of 'dry' in this context is worth careful study

190 *dint* blow, impact

191–2 note the change of language to suggest the change of scene. Liquid l's and m's replace hard consonants; long slow words replace short, sharp ones

193 *dusky* dark-ish. But the word seems inept in view of the next line

194 *funeral scarf* black silk or crêpe worn by mourners at a funeral

197 *black-stoled* wearing black robes

198 *Three Queens* see *Notes*

199 *tingling* vibrating. But the word is meaningless apart from its phrase—'shiver'd to the tingling stars.' We know just what Tennyson meant although it defies detailed explanation

Of lamentation, like a wind, that shrills
All night in a waste land, where no one comes,
Or hath come, since the making of the world.
  Then murmur'd Arthur, 'Place me in the barge,'
And to the barge they came. There those three Queens   20
Put forth their hands, and took the King, and wept.
But she, that rose the tallest of them all
And fairest, laid his head upon her lap,
And loosed the shatter'd casque, and chafed his hands,
And call'd him by his name, complaining loud,   21
And dropping bitter tears against his brow
Striped with dark blood: for all his face was white
And colourless, and like the wither'd moon
Smote by the fresh beam of the springing east;
And all his greaves and cuisses dash'd with drops   21
Of onset; and the light and lustrous curls—
That made his forehead like a rising sun
High from the daïs-throne—were parch'd with dust;
Or, clotted into points and hanging loose,
Mix'd with the knightly growth that fringed his lips.   22
So like a shatter'd column lay the King;
Not like that Arthur who, with lance in rest,
From spur to plume a star of tournament,
Shot thro' the lists at Camelot, and charged
Before the eyes of ladies and of kings.   22
  Then loudly cried the bold Sir Bedivere,
'Ah! my Lord Arthur, whither shall I go?
Where shall I hide my forehead and my eyes?
For now I see the true old times are dead,
When every morning brought a noble chance,   23
And every chance brought out a noble knight.

215 *greaves and cuisses* armour for shins and thighs
215–16 *drops of onset* blood from the battle
219–20 are these two lines in keeping with the rest of the poem?

Such times have been not since the light that led
The holy Elders with the gift of myrrh.
But now the whole ROUND TABLE is dissolved
Which was an image of the mighty world; 235
And I, the last, go forth companionless,
And the days darken round me, and the years,
Among new men, strange faces, other minds.'
And slowly answered Arthur from the barge:
'The old order changeth, yielding place to new, 240
And God fulfils Himself in many ways,
Lest one good custom should corrupt the world.
Comfort thyself: what comfort is in me?
I have lived my life, and that which I have done,
May He within Himself make pure! but thou, 245
If thou shouldst never see my face again,
Pray for my soul. More things are wrought by prayer
Than this world dreams of. Wherefore, let thy voice
Rise like a fountain for me night and day.
For what are men better than sheep or goats 250
That nourish a blind life within the brain,
If, knowing God, they lift not hands of prayer
Both for themselves and those who call them friend?
For so the whole round earth is every way
Bound by gold chains about the feet of God. 255
But now farewell. I am going a long way
With these thou seëst—if indeed I go—
(For all my mind is clouded with a doubt)
To the island-valley of Avilion;
Where falls not hail, or rain, or any snow, 260
Nor ever wind blows loudly; but it lies
Deep-meadow'd, happy fair with orchard-lawns

259 *Avilion* or Avalon. A mythical land. Attempts to identify it with Glastonbury are not very convincing

And bowery hollows crown'd with summer sea,
Where I will heal me of my grievous wound.'
 So said he, and the barge with oar and sail 26
Moved from the brink, like some full-breasted swan
That, fluting a wild carol ere her death,
Ruffles her pure cold plume, and takes the flood
With swarthy webs. Long stood Sir Bedivere
Revolving many memories, till the hull 27
Look'd one black dot against the verge of dawn,
And on the mere the wailing died away.

Dora

WITH farmer Allan at the farm abode
William and Dora. William was his son,
And she his niece. He often look'd at them,
And often thought, 'I'll make them man and wife.'
Now Dora felt her uncle's will in all,
And yearn'd toward William; but the youth, because
He had been always with her in the house,
Thought not of Dora.
 Then there came a day
When Allan call'd his son, and said, 'My son:
I married late, but I would wish to see
My grandchild on my knees before I die:
And I have set my heart upon a match.
Now therefore look to Dora; she is well
To look to; thrifty too beyond her age.
She is my brother's daughter: he and I
Had once hard words, and parted, and he died

267 a reference to the belief—kept alive, possibly by the word 'swan-song'—that swans, whose normal 'song' is scarcely pleasing, sing beautifully just before they die

In foreign lands; but for his sake I bred
His daughter Dora: take her for your wife;
For I have wish'd this marriage, night and day,
For many years.' But William answer'd short; 20
'I cannot marry Dora; by my life,
I will not marry Dora.' Then the old man
Was wroth, and doubled up his hands, and said:
'You will not, boy! you dare to answer thus!
But in my time a father's word was law, 25
And so it shall be now for me. Look to it;
Consider, William: take a month to think,
And let me have an answer to my wish;
Or, by the Lord that made me, you shall pack,
And never more darken my doors again.' 30
But William answer'd madly; bit his lips,
And broke away. The more he look'd at her
The less he liked her; and his ways were harsh;
But Dora bore them meekly. Then before
The month was out he left his father's house, 35
And hired himself to work within the fields;
And half in love, half spite, he woo'd and wed
A labourer's daughter, Mary Morrison.
   Then, when the bells were ringing, Allan call'd
His niece and said: 'My girl, I love you well; 40
But if you speak with him that was my son,
Or change a word with her he calls his wife,
My home is none of yours. My will is law.'
And Dora promised, being meek. She thought,
'It cannot be: my uncle's mind will change!' 45
   And days went on, and there was born a boy
To William; then distresses came on him;
And day by day he pass'd his father's gate,

42 *change* exchange

Heart-broken, and his father help'd him not.
But Dora stored what little she could save, 50
And sent it them by stealth, nor did they know
Who sent it; till at last a fever seized
On William, and in harvest time he died.
  Then Dora went to Mary. Mary sat
And look'd with tears upon her boy, and thought 55
Hard things of Dora. Dora came and said:
  'I have obey'd my uncle until now,
And I have sinn'd, for it was all thro' me
This evil came on William at the first.
But, Mary, for the sake of him that's gone, 60
And for your sake, the woman that he chose,
And for this orphan, I am come to you:
You know there has not been for these five years
So full a harvest: let me take the boy,
And I will set him in my uncle's eye 65
Among the wheat; that when his heart is glad
Of the full harvest, he may see the boy,
And bless him for the sake of him that's gone.'
  And Dora took the child, and went her way
Across the wheat, and sat upon a mound 70
That was unsown, where many poppies grew.
Far off the farmer came into the field
And spied her not; for none of all his men
Dare tell him Dora waited with the child;
And Dora would have risen and gone to him, 75
But her heart fail'd her; and the reapers reap'd,
And the sun fell, and all the land was dark.
  But when the morrow came, she rose and took
The child once more, and sat upon the mound;
And made a little wreath of all the flowers 80
That grew about, and tied it round his hat
To make him pleasing in her uncle's eye.

Then when the farmer pass'd into the field
He spied her, and he left his men at work,
And came and said: 'Where were you yesterday? 85
Whose child is that? What are you doing here?'
So Dora cast her eyes upon the ground,
And answer'd softly, 'This is William's child!'
'And did I not,' said Allan, 'did I not
Forbid you, Dora?' Dora said again: 90
'Do with me as you will, but take the child,
And bless him for the sake of him that's gone!'
And Allan said, 'I see it is a trick
Got up betwixt you and the woman there.
I must be taught my duty, and by you! 95
You knew my word was law, and yet you dared
To slight it. Well—for I will take the boy;
But go you hence, and never see me more.'
So saying, he took the boy that cried aloud
And struggled hard. The wreath of flowers fell 100
At Dora's feet. She bow'd upon her hands,
And the boy's cry came to her from the field,
More and more distant. She bow'd down her head,
Remembering the day when first she came,
And all the things that had been. She bow'd down 105
And wept in secret; and the reapers reap'd,
And the sun fell, and all the land was dark.
Then Dora went to Mary's house, and stood
Upon the threshold. Mary saw the boy
Was not with Dora. She broke out in praise 110
To God, that help'd her in her widowhood.
And Dora said, 'My uncle took the boy;
But, Mary, let me live and work with you:
He says that he will never see me more.'
Then answer'd Mary, 'This shall never be, 115
That thou shouldst take my trouble on thyself:

And, now I think, he shall not have the boy,
For he will teach him hardness, and to slight
His mother; therefore thou and I will go,
And I will have my boy, and bring him home; 120
And I will beg of him to take thee back:
But if he will not take thee back again,
Then thou and I will live within one house,
And work for William's child, until he grows
Of age to help us.'

So the women kiss'd 125
Each other, and set out, and reach'd the farm.
The door was off the latch: they peep'd, and saw
The boy set up betwixt his grandsire's knees,
Who thrust him in the hollows of his arm,
And clapt him on the hands and on the cheeks, 130
Like one that loved him: and the lad stretch'd out
And babbled for the golden seal, that hung
From Allan's watch, and sparkled by the fire.
Then they came in: but when the boy beheld
His mother, he cried out to come to her: 135
And Allan set him down, and Mary said:

'O Father!—if you let me call you so—
I never came a-begging for myself,
Or William, or this child; but now I come
For Dora: take her back; she loves you well. 140
O Sir, when William died, he died at peace
With all men; for I ask'd him, and he said,
He could not ever rue his marrying me—
I had been a patient wife: but, Sir, he said
That he was wrong to cross his father thus: 145
"God bless him!" he said, "and may he never know
The troubles I have gone thro'!" Then he turn'd
His face and pass'd—unhappy that I am!
But now, Sir, let me have my boy, for you

Will make him hard, and he will learn to slight 150
His father's memory; and take Dora back,
And let all this be as it was before.'
So Mary said, and Dora hid her face
By Mary. There was silence in the room;
And all at once the old man burst in sobs:— 155
'I have been to blame—to blame. I have kill'd my son.
I have kill'd him—but I loved him—my dear son.
May God forgive me!—I have been to blame.
Kiss me, my children.'
Then they clung about
The old man's neck, and kiss'd him many times. 160
And all the man was broken with remorse;
And all his love came back a hundredfold;
And for three hours he sobb'd o'er William's child
Thinking of William.
So those four abode
Within one house together; and as years 165
Went forward, Mary took another mate;
But Dora lived unmarried till her death.

Audley Court

'THE Bull, the Fleece are cramm'd, and not a room
For love or money. Let us picnic there
At Audley Court.'
I spoke, while Audley feast
Humm'd like a hive all round the narrow quay,
To Francis, with a basket on his arm, 5

1 as the party had brought a picnic meal with them the reference to the hotels is difficult to understand

3 *Audley feast* a local fair, apparently. The scene, although suggested by Torquay (see *Notes*), is imaginary

To Francis just alighted from the boat,
And breathing of the sea. 'With all my heart,'
Said Francis. Then we shoulder'd thro' the swarm,
And rounded by the stillness of the beach
To where the bay runs up its latest horn. 10
We left the dying ebb that faintly lipp'd
The flat red granite; so by many a sweep
Of meadow smooth from aftermath we reach'd
The griffin-guarded gates, and pass'd thro' all
The pillar'd dusk of sounding sycamores, 15
And cross'd the garden to the gardener's lodge,
With all its casements bedded, and its walls
And chimneys muffled in the leafy vine.
There, on a slope of orchard, Francis laid
A damask napkin wrought with horse and hound, 20
Brought out a dusky loaf that smelt of home,
And, half-cut-down, a pasty costly-made,
Where quail and pigeon, lark and leveret lay,
Like fossils of the rock, with golden yolks
Imbedded and injellied; last, with these, 25
A flask of cider from his father's vats,
Prime, which I knew; and so we sat and eat
And talk'd old matters over; who was dead,
Who married, who was like to be, and how
The races went, and who would rent the hall: 30
Then touch'd upon the game, how scarce it was
This season; glancing thence, discuss'd the farm,
The four-field system, and the price of grain;
And struck upon the corn-laws, where we split,

13 *smooth from aftermath* after the last of the hay harvest had been gleaned
17 *bedded* set in flower-beds
27 *eat* Victorian past tense (as well as present)
34 *struck upon* came round to discussing
split disagreed

And came again together on the king 35
With heated faces; till he laugh'd aloud;
And, while the blackbird on the pippin hung
To hear him, clapt his hand in mine and sang—
'Oh! who would fight and march and countermarch,
Be shot for sixpence in a battle-field, 40
And shovell'd up into some bloody trench
Where no one knows? but let me live my life.
'Oh! who would cast and balance at a desk,
Perch'd like a crow upon a three-legg'd stool,
Till all his juice is dried, and all his joints 45
Are full of chalk? but let me live my life.
'Who'd serve the state? for if I carved my name
Upon the cliffs that guard my native land,
I might as well have traced it in the sands;
The sea wastes all: but let me live my life. 50
'Oh! who would love? I woo'd a woman once,
But she was sharper than an eastern wind,
And all my heart turn'd from her, as a thorn
Turns from the sea; but let me live my life.'
He sang his song, and I replied with mine: 55
I found it in a volume, all of songs,
Knock'd down to me, when old Sir Robert's pride,
His books—the more the pity, so I said—
Came to the hammer here in March—and this—
I set the words, and added names I knew. 60
'Sleep, Ellen Aubrey, sleep, and dream of me:

35 *the king* no particular king, of course (Queen Victoria was already on the British throne)

43 *cast and balance* figures in a ledger

53–4 *as a thorn / Turns from the sea* why does a thorn (i.e. thorn bush) turn from the sea?

58 the speaker thought it a pity that Sir Robert's books should have been his pride, not that they 'came to the hammer'

Sleep, Ellen, folded in thy sister's arm,
And sleeping, haply dream her arm is mine.
'Sleep, Ellen, folded in Emilia's arm;
Emilia, fairer than all else but thou, 65
For thou art fairer than all else that is.
'Sleep, breathing health and peace upon her breast:
Sleep, breathing love and trust against her lip:
I go to-night: I come to-morrow morn.
'I go, but I return: I would I were 70
The pilot of the darkness and the dream.
Sleep, Ellen Aubrey, love, and dream of me.'
So sang we each to either, Francis Hale,
The farmer's son, who lived across the bay,
My friend; and I, that having wherewithal, 75
And in the fallow leisure of my life
A rolling stone of here and everywhere,
Did what I would; but ere the night we rose
And saunter'd home beneath a moon, that, just
In crescent, dimly rain'd about the leaf 80
Twilights of airy silver, till we reach'd
The limit of the hills; and as we sank
From rock to rock upon the glooming quay,
The town was hush'd beneath us: lower down
The bay was oily calm; the harbour-buoy, 85
Sole star of phosphorescence in the calm,
With one green sparkle ever and anon
Dipt by itself, and we were glad at heart.

65 this line repays a little close study

75 *having wherewithal* having 'the necessary,' i.e., comfortably off

76 *fallow* idle

78–88 see *Notes*. Compare the poetry of these lines with what has preceded them

Ulysses

It little profits that an idle king,
By this still hearth, among these barren crags,
Match'd with an aged wife, I mete and dole
Unequal laws unto a savage race,
That hoard, and sleep, and feed, and know not me. 5
I cannot rest from travel: I will drink
Life to the lees: all times I have enjoy'd
Greatly, have suffer'd greatly, both with those
That loved me, and alone; on shore, and when
Thro' scudding drifts the rainy Hyades 10
Vext the dim sea: I am become a name;
For always roaming with a hungry heart
Much have I seen and known; cities of men
And manners, climates, councils, governments,
Myself not least, but honour'd of them all; 15
And drunk delight of battle with my peers,
Far on the ringing plains of windy Troy.
I am a part of all that I have met;
Yet all experience is an arch wherethro'
Gleams that untravell'd world, whose margin fades 20
For ever and for ever when I move.

3 *mete* measure out

3–5 the lines suggest that Ulysses holds a poor opinion of the people of Ithaca, over whom he rules. Even his own laws seem 'unequal' in his jaundiced view

7 *lees* dregs

10 *rainy Hyades* the Hyades were seven daughters of Atlas who died of sorrow at the death of their brother, Hyas. They became a group of stars which foretold rain if they appeared in the heavens at dawn. (Not to be confused with the Pleiades, who were seven other daughters of Atlas)

16 *peers* equals

20 *margin* border

How dull it is to pause, to make an end,
To rust unburnish'd, not to shine in use!
As tho' to breathe were life. Life piled on life
Were all too little, and of one to me 25
Little remains: but every hour is saved
From that eternal silence, something more,
A bringer of new things; and vile it were
For some three suns to store and hoard myself,
And this gray spirit yearning in desire 30
To follow knowledge like a sinking star,
Beyond the utmost bound of human thought.
This is my son, mine own Telemachus,
To whom I leave the sceptre and the isle—
Well-loved of me, discerning to fulfil 35
This labour, by slow prudence to make mild
A rugged people, and thro' soft degrees
Subdue them to the useful and the good.
Most blameless is he, centred in the sphere
Of common duties, decent not to fail 40
In offices of tenderness, and pay
Meet adoration to my household gods,
When I am gone. He works his work, I mine.
There lies the port; the vessel puffs her sail:
There gloom the dark broad seas. My mariners, 45
Souls that have toil'd, and wrought, and thought with me—
That ever with a frolic welcome took
The thunder and the sunshine, and opposed

25 *of one* of one life

26 *every hour* this is an adverbial phrase. 'Something more' (l. 27) is saved every hour

29 *suns* years. Ulysses apparently gives himself about three more years to live

35–36 *discerning to fulfil / This labour* with the intelligence to complete my work

40 *decent* suitable, to be relied on

Free hearts, free foreheads—you and I are old;
Old age hath yet his honour and his toil; 50
Death closes all: but something ere the end,
Some work of noble note, may yet be done,
Not unbecoming men that strove with Gods.
The lights begin to twinkle from the rocks:
The long day wanes: the slow moon climbs: the deep 55
Moans round with many voices. Come, my friends,
'Tis not too late to seek a newer world.
Push off, and sitting well in order smite
The sounding furrows; for my purpose holds
To sail beyond the sunset, and the baths 60
Of all the western stars, until I die.
It may be that the gulfs will wash us down:
It may be we shall touch the Happy Isles,
And see the great Achilles, whom we knew.
Tho' much is taken, much abides; and tho' 65
We are not now that strength which in old days
Moved earth and heaven; that which we are, we are;
One equal temper of heroic hearts,
Made weak by time and fate, but strong in will
To strive, to seek, to find, and not to yield. 70

Locksley Hall

COMRADES, leave me here a little, while as yet 'tis early morn:
Leave me here, and when you want me, sound upon the bugle-horn.

63 *the Happy Isles* somewhere beyond the (present) Straits of Gibraltar lay the mythical islands of the blest, where departed souls lived in a sort of happy retirement

64 *Achilles, whom we knew* Ulysses and Achilles were together in the Trojan war

68 *temper* temperament, disposition. What figure of speech is this?

'Tis the place, and all around it, as of old, the curlews call,
Dreary gleams about the moorland flying over Locksley Hall;

Locksley Hall, that in the distance overlooks the sandy tracts, 5
And the hollow ocean-ridges roaring into cataracts.

Many a night from yonder ivied casement, ere I went to rest,
Did I look on great Orion sloping slowly to the West.

Many a night I saw the Pleiads, rising thro' the mellow shade,
Glitter like a swarm of fire-flies tangled in a silver braid. 10

Here about the beach I wander'd, nourishing a youth sublime
With the fairy tales of science, and the long result of Time;

When the centuries behind me like a fruitful land reposed;
When I clung to all the present for the promise that it closed:

When I dipt into the future far as human eye could see; 15
Saw the Vision of the world, and all the wonder that would be.—

In the Spring a fuller crimson comes upon the robin's breast;
In the Spring the wanton lapwing gets himself another crest;

In the Spring a livelier iris changes on the burnish'd dove;
In the Spring a young man's fancy lightly turns to thoughts of
love. 20

Then her cheek was pale and thinner than should be for one so
young,
And her eyes on all my motions with a mute observance hung.

4 *gleams* a noun, subject of the verb *flying*, *i.e.* as they fly
9–10 find the Pleiades on a starry night and test the accuracy and vividness of this description

And I said, 'My cousin Amy, speak, and speak the truth to me,
Trust me, cousin, all the current of my being sets to thee.'

On her pallid cheek and forehead came a colour and a light, 25
As I have seen the rosy red flushing in the northern night.

And she turn'd—her bosom shaken with a sudden storm of sighs—
All the spirit deeply dawning in the dark of hazel eyes—

Saying, 'I have hid my feelings, fearing they should do me wrong;'
Saying, 'Dost thou love me, cousin?' weeping, 'I have loved thee long.' 30

Love took up the glass of Time, and turn'd it in his glowing hands;
Every moment, lightly shaken, ran itself in golden sands.

Love took up the harp of Life, and smote on all the chords with might;
Smote the chord of Self, that, trembling, pass'd in music out of sight.

Many a morning on the moorland did we hear the copses ring, 35
And her whisper throng'd my pulses with the fulness of the Spring.

Many an evening by the waters did we watch the stately ships,
And our spirits rush'd together at the touching of the lips.

O my cousin, shallow-hearted! O my Amy, mine no more!
O the dreary, dreary moorland! O the barren, barren shore! 40

26 a reference to the Aurora Borealis

Falser than all fancy fathoms, falser than all songs have sung,
Puppet to a father's threat, and servile to a shrewish tongue!

Is it well to wish thee happy?—having known me—to decline
On a range of lower feelings and a narrower heart than mine!

Yet it shall be: thou shalt lower to his level day by day, 45
What is fine within thee growing coarse to sympathise with clay.

As the husband is, the wife is: thou art mated with a clown,
And the grossness of his nature will have weight to drag thee
down.

He will hold thee, when his passion shall have spent its novel
force,
Something better than his dog, a little dearer than his horse. 50

What is this? his eyes are heavy: think not they are glazed with
wine.
Go to him: it is thy duty: kiss him: take his hand in thine.

It may be my lord is weary, that his brain is overwrought:
Soothe him with thy finer fancies, touch him with thy lighter
thought.

He will answer to the purpose, easy things to understand— 55
Better thou wert dead before me, tho' I slew thee with my hand!

Better thou and I were lying, hidden from the heart's disgrace,
Roll'd in one another's arms, and silent in a last embrace.

Cursed be the social wants that sin against the strength of youth!
Cursed be the social lies that warp us from the living truth! 60

41 *fathoms* a verb, falser than imagination can measure
59 *the social wants* the demands of society

Cursed be the sickly forms that err from honest Nature's rule!
Cursed be the gold that gilds the straiten'd forehead of the fool!

Well—'tis well that I should bluster!—Hadst thou less unworthy proved—
Would to God—for I had loved thee more than ever wife was loved.

Am I mad, that I should cherish that which bears but bitter fruit? 65
I will pluck it from my bosom, tho' my heart be at the root.

Never, tho' my mortal summers to such length of years should come
As the many-winter'd crow that leads the clanging rookery home.

Where is comfort? in division of the records of the mind?
Can I part her from herself, and love her, as I knew her, kind? 70

I remember one that perish'd: sweetly did she speak and move:
Such a one do I remember, whom to look at was to love.

Can I think of her as dead, and love her for the love she bore?
No—she never loved me truly: love is love for evermore.

Comfort? comfort scorn'd of devils! this is truth the poet sings, 75
That a sorrow's crown of sorrow is remembering happier things.

Drug thy memories, lest thou learn it, lest thy heart be put to proof,
In the dead unhappy night, and when the rain is on the roof.

62 *the straiten'd forehead* the low brow. The lover is smarting under the injustice which allows wealth to provide a compensation for stupidity
69 *in division . . . mind?* can I gain comfort by remembering only the pleasant things about her? (i.e. splitting up my memories)

Like a dog, he hunts in dreams, and thou art starting at the wall,
Where the dying night-lamp flickers, and the shadows rise and
fall. 80

Then a hand shall pass before thee, pointing to his drunken sleep,
To thy widow'd marriage-pillows, to the tears that thou wilt
weep.

Thou shalt hear the 'Never, never,' whisper'd by the phantom
years,
And a song from out the distance in the ringing of thine ears;

And an eye shall vex thee, looking ancient kindness on thy pain. 85
Turn thee, turn thee on thy pillow: get thee to thy rest again.

Nay, but Nature brings thee solace; for a tender voice will cry.
'Tis a purer life than thine; a lip to drain thy trouble dry.

Baby lips will laugh me down: my latest rival brings thee rest.
Baby fingers, waxen touches, press me from the mother's breast. 90

O, the child too clothes the father with a dearness not his due.
Half is thine and half is his: it will be worthy of the two.

O, I see thee old and formal, fitted to thy petty part,
With a little hoard of maxims preaching down a daughter's heart.

'They were dangerous guides the feelings—she herself was not
exempt— 95
Truly, she herself had suffer'd'—Perish in thy self-contempt!

Overlive it—lower yet—be happy! wherefore should I care?
I myself must mix with action, lest I wither by despair.

95–6 he imagines the mother telling her story, in the third person, to her daughter
97 *Overlive it* live it down

What is that which I should turn to, lighting upon days like these?
Every door is barr'd with gold, and opens but to golden keys. 100

Every gate is throng'd with suitors, all the markets overflow.
I have but an angry fancy: what is that which I should do?

I had been content to perish, falling on the foeman's ground,
When the ranks are roll'd in vapour, and the winds are laid with
sound.

But the jingling of the guinea helps the hurt that Honour feels, 105
And the nations do but murmur, snarling at each other's heels.

Can I but relive in sadness? I will turn that earlier page.
Hide me from my deep emotion, O thou wondrous Mother-Age!

Make me feel the wild pulsation that I felt before the strife,
When I heard my days before me, and the tumult of my life; 110

Yearning for the large excitement that the coming years would
yield,
Eager-hearted as a boy when first he leaves his father's field,

And at night along the dusky highway near and nearer drawn,
Sees in heaven the light of London flaring like a dreary dawn;

And his spirit leaps within him to be gone before him then, 115
Underneath the light he looks at, in among the throngs of men:

103–6 he would have welcomed the chance to die in battle, but there are no wars. Nations are insulted but their grievances are assuaged by money and they 'do but murmur'

107 will sadness allow me to recapture life? I will turn back the page of youth (and therefore hope)

108 *Mother-Age* the days of his youth will be like a mother to him, protecting him from his deep despair

Men, my brothers, men the workers, ever reaping something
new:
That which they have done but earnest of the things that they
shall do:

For I dipt into the future, far as human eye could see,
Saw the Vision of the world, and all the wonder that would be; 12

Saw the heavens fill with commerce, argosies of magic sails,
Pilots of the purple twilight, dropping down with costly bales;

Heard the heavens fill with shouting, and there rain'd a ghastly
dew
From the nations' airy navies grappling in the central blue;

Far along the world-wide whisper of the south-wind rushing
warm, 12
With the standards of the peoples plunging thro' the thunder-
storm;

Till the war-drum throbb'd no longer, and the battle-flags were
furl'd
In the Parliament of man, the Federation of the world.

There the common sense of most shall hold a fretful realm in
awe,
And the kindly earth shall slumber, lapt in universal law. 13

So I triumph'd ere my passion sweeping thro' me left me dry,
Left me with the palsied heart, and left me with the jaundiced
eye;

118 *earnest* foretaste

121 *argosies* fleets (from Ragusa, now Dubrovnik, a wealthy city of the 15th and 16th centuries, whose fleets sailed the world with rich merchandise)

Eye, to which all order festers, all things here are out of joint:
Science moves, but slowly slowly, creeping on from point to point:

Slowly comes a hungry people, as a lion creeping nigher, 135
Glares at one that nods and winks behind a slowly-dying fire.

Yet I doubt not thro' the ages one increasing purpose runs,
And the thoughts of men are widen'd with the process of the suns.

What is that to him that reaps not harvest of his youthful joys,
Tho' the deep heart of existence beat for ever like a boy's? 140

Knowledge comes, but wisdom lingers, and I linger on the shore,
And the individual withers, and the world is more and more.

Knowledge comes, but wisdom lingers, and he bears a laden breast,
Full of sad experience, moving toward the stillness of his rest.

Hark, my merry comrades call me, sounding on the bugle-horn, 145
They to whom my foolish passion were a target for their scorn:

Shall it not be scorn to me to harp on such a moulder'd string?
I am shamed thro' all my nature to have loved so slight a thing.

142 if this was Tennyson's view when he wrote *Locksley Hall* he lived to change it. He grew more and more to look for the salvation of mankind in individual great men; less and less to pin his faith on mankind as a whole (see *Notes* to *Ode on the Death of the Duke of Wellington*)

is more and more has more and more power and influence

146 *were* (subjunctive) would be if they knew about it

Weakness to be wroth with weakness! woman's pleasure, woman's pain—
Nature made them blinder motions bounded in a shallower brain:

Woman is the lesser man, and all thy passions, match'd with mine,
Are as moonlight unto sunlight, and as water unto wine—

Here at least, where nature sickens, nothing. Ah, for some retreat
Deep in yonder shining Orient, where my life began to beat;

Where in wild Mahratta-battle fell my father evil-starr'd;—
I was left a trampled orphan, and a selfish uncle's ward.

Or to burst all links of habit—there to wander far away,
On from island unto island at the gateways of the day.

Larger constellations burning, mellow moons and happy skies,
Breadths of tropic shade and palms in cluster, knots of Paradise.

Never comes the trader, never floats an European flag,
Slides the bird o'er lustrous woodland, swings the trailer from the crag;

Droops the heavy-blossom'd bower, hangs the heavy-fruited tree—
Summer isles of Eden lying in dark-purple spheres of sea.

149–52 this view—of woman's inferiority to man—was later flatly contradicted in *The Princess*

155 *Mahratta* a warlike people in the Bombay region of India; subdued about 1818 by the East India Company

162 *the trailer* trailing creeper

There methinks would be enjoyment more than in this march of mind, 165
In the steamship, in the railway, in the thoughts that shake mankind.

There the passions cramp'd no longer shall have scope and breathing space;
I will take some savage woman, she shall rear my dusky race.

Iron jointed, supple-sinew'd, they shall dive, and they shall run,
Catch the wild goat by the hair, and hurl their lances in the sun; 170

Whistle back the parrot's call, and leap the rainbows of the brooks,
Not with blinded eyesight poring over miserable books—

Fool, again the dream, the fancy! but I *know* my words are wild,
But I count the gray barbarian lower than the Christian child.

I, to herd with narrow foreheads, vacant of our glorious gains, 175
Like a beast with lower pleasures, like a beast with lower pains!

Mated with a squalid savage—what to me were sun or clime?
I the heir of all the ages, in the foremost files of time—

I that rather held it better men should perish one by one,
Than that earth should stand at gaze like Joshua's moon in Ajalon! 180

175 *vacant of our glorious gains* knowing nothing of the glorious triumphs of (Western) civilisation
178 *files* ranks
180 Joshua commanded the sun and moon to stand still, the sun upon Gibeon and the moon 'in the valley of Ajalon' while the Israelites defeated their enemies (*Joshua* x, 12, 13)

Not in vain the distance beacons. Forward, forward let us range,
Let the great world spin for ever down the ringing grooves of
change.

Thro' the shadow of the globe we sweep into the younger day:
Better fifty years of Europe than a cycle of Cathay.

Mother-Age (for mine I knew not) help me as when life begun:
Rift the hills, and roll the waters, flash the lightnings, weigh the
Sun.

O, I see the crescent promise of my spirit hath not set.
Ancient founts of inspiration well thro' all my fancy yet.

Howsoever these things be, a long farewell to Locksley Hall!
Now for me the woods may wither, now for me the roof-tree fall.

Comes a vapour from the margin, blackening over heath and holt,
Cramming all the blast before it, in its breast a thunderbolt.

Let it fall on Locksley Hall, with rain or hail, or fire or snow;
For the mighty wind arises, roaring seaward, and I go.

182 *ringing grooves* Tennyson travelled in the first train from Liverpool to Manchester in 1830. There was a great crowd and he did not see the railway lines in the dark. He therefore thought that the train wheels ran in grooves and it was some years before he learnt otherwise

184 *a cycle of Cathay* an age of (life in) China. The cycle was the name used by astronomers to denote the period in which a heavenly body, e.g., a comet, completes its orbit. Tennyson first used the word in this sense

187 *crescent* growing, like the crescent moon

188 *well* spring up

190 *for me* for all me

191 *a vapour from the margin* a great cloud from the direction of the sea-shore

holt a small wood

Tithonus

The woods decay, the woods decay and fall,
The vapours weep their burthen to the ground,
Man comes and tills the field and lies beneath,
And after many a summer dies the swan.
Me only cruel immortality 5
Consumes: I wither slowly in thine arms,
Here at the quiet limit of the world,
A white-hair'd shadow roaming like a dream
The ever-silent spaces of the East,
Far-folded mists, and gleaming halls of morn. 10

Alas! for this gray shadow, once a man—
So glorious in his beauty and thy choice,
Who madest him thy chosen, that he seem'd
To his great heart none other than a God!
I ask'd thee, 'Give me immortality.' 15
Then didst thou grant mine asking with a smile,
Like wealthy men who care not how they give.
But thy strong Hours indignant work'd their wills,
And beat me down and marr'd and wasted me,
And tho' they could not end me, left me maim'd 20
To dwell in presence of immortal youth,
Immortal age beside immortal youth,
And all I was, in ashes. Can thy love,
Thy beauty, make amends, tho' even now,
Close over us, the silver star, thy guide, 25
Shines in those tremulous eyes that fill with tears
To hear me? Let me go: take back thy gift:

6 *thine* Aurora's
9 why 'the East'?
18 *indignant* presumably because the natural order had been upset by his having been made immortal
25 *Close* an adjective here, not a verb

Why should a man desire in any way
To vary from the kindly race of men,
Or pass beyond the goal of ordinance
Where all should pause, as is most meet for all?

A soft air fans the cloud apart; there comes
A glimpse of that dark world where I was born.
Once more the old mysterious glimmer steals
From thy pure brows, and from thy shoulders pure,
And bosom beating with a heart renew'd.
Thy cheek begins to redden thro' the gloom,
Thy sweet eyes brighten slowly close to mine,
Ere yet they blind the stars, and the wild team
Which love thee, yearning for thy yoke, arise,
And shake the darkness from their loosen'd manes,
And beat the twilight into flakes of fire.

Lo! ever thus thou growest beautiful
In silence, then before thine answer given
Departest, and thy tears are on my cheek.

Why wilt thou ever scare me with thy tears,
And make me tremble lest a saying learnt,
In days far-off, on that dark earth, be true?
'The Gods themselves cannot recall their gifts.'

Ay me! ay me! with what another heart
In days far-off, and with what other eyes
I used to watch—if I be he that watch'd—
The lucid outline forming round thee; saw
The dim curls kindle into sunny rings;
Changed with thy mystic change, and felt my blood
Glow with the glow that slowly crimson'd all

30 *goal of ordinance* ordained limit
39–40 a reference to the horses that drove the chariot of the Dawn

Thy presence and thy portals, while I lay,
Mouth, forehead, eyelids, growing dewy-warm
With kisses balmier than half-opening buds
Of April, and could hear the lips that kiss'd 60
Whispering I knew not what of wild and sweet,
Like that strange song I heard Apollo sing,
While Ilion like a mist rose into towers.

Yet hold me not for ever in thine East:
How can my nature longer mix with thine? 65
Coldly thy rosy shadows bathe me, cold
Are all thy lights, and cold my wrinkled feet
Upon thy glimmering thresholds, when the steam
Floats up from those dim fields about the homes
Of happy men that have the power to die, 70
And grassy barrows of the happier dead.
Release me, and restore me to the ground;
Thou seëst all things, thou wilt see my grave:
Thou wilt renew thy beauty morn by morn;
I earth in earth forget these empty courts, 75
And thee returning on thy silver wheels.

A Farewell

FLOW down, cold rivulet, to the sea,
Thy tribute wave deliver:
No more by thee my steps shall be,
For ever and for ever.

59 *balmier* more fragrant, as well as more soothing
62–3 see Note to *Œnone*, ll. 39–40
63 *Ilion* Troy
71 *barrows* burial-mounds
75 *earth in earth* dead and buried
76 *silver wheels* the wheels of Aurora's chariot

Flow, softly flow, by lawn and lea,
A rivulet then a river:
No where by thee my steps shall be,
For ever and for ever.

But here will sigh thine alder tree,
And here thine aspen shiver;
And here by thee will hum the bee,
For ever and for ever.

A thousand suns will stream on thee,
A thousand moons will quiver;
But not by thee my steps shall be,
For ever and for ever.

The Eagle

FRAGMENT

He clasps the crag with crooked hands;
Close to the sun in lonely lands,
Ring'd with the azure world, he stands.

The wrinkled sea beneath him crawls;
He watches from his mountain walls,
And like a thunderbolt he falls.

Break, Break, Break

Break, break, break,
On thy cold gray stones, O Sea!
And I would that my tongue could utter
The thoughts that arise in me.

O well for the fisherman's boy,
  That he shouts with his sister at play!
O well for the sailor lad,
  That he sings in his boat on the bay! 5

And the stately ships go on
  To their haven under the hill; 10
But O for the touch of a vanish'd hand,
  And the sound of a voice that is still!

Break, break, break,
  At the foot of thy crags, O Sea!
But the tender grace of a day that is dead 15
  Will never come back to me.

The Poet's Song

THE rain had fallen, the Poet arose,
  He pass'd by the town and out of the street,
A light wind blew from the gates of the sun,
  And waves of shadow went over the wheat,
And he sat him down in a lonely place, 5
  And chanted a melody loud and sweet,
That made the wild-swan pause in her cloud,
  And the lark drop down at his feet.

The swallow stopt as he hunted the fly,
  The snake slipt under a spray, 10
The wild hawk stood with the down on his beak,
  And stared, with his foot on the prey,
And the nightingale thought, 'I have sung many songs,
  But never a one so gay,
For he sings of what the world will be 15
  When the years have died away.'

The Brook

HERE, by this brook, we parted; I to the East
And he for Italy—too late—too late:
One whom the strong sons of the world despise;
For lucky rhymes to him were scrip and share,
And mellow metres more than cent for cent; 5
Nor could he understand how money breeds,
Thought it a dead thing; yet himself could make
The thing that is not as the thing that is.
O had he lived! In our schoolbooks we say,
Of those that held their heads above the crowd, 10
They flourish'd then or then; but life in him
Could scarce be said to flourish, only touch'd
On such a time as goes before the leaf,
When all the wood stands in a mist of green,
And nothing perfect: yet the brook he loved, 15
For which, in branding summers of Bengal,
Or ev'n the sweet half-English Neilgherry air
I panted, seems, as I re-listen to it,
Prattling the primrose fancies of the boy,
To me that loved him; for 'O brook,' he says, 20
'O babbling brook,' says Edmund in his rhyme,
'Whence come you?' and the brook, why not? replies.

I come from haunts of coot and hern,
I make a sudden sally,
And sparkle out among the fern, 25
To bicker down a valley.

1, 2 *we . . . I . . . he* 'I' is Lawrence Aylmer (l. 197); 'he' is his brother Edmund, a poet. Lawrence has returned to his old home, adjoining 'Philip's farm' after twenty years in India

4, 5 *scrip and share . . . cent for cent* the language of the Stock-Exchange

17 *Neilgherry* more usually Nilgiri (Hills), a district in S. India with a delightful 'English' climate

19 why '*primrose* fancies'?

By thirty hills I hurry down,
  Or slip between the ridges,
By twenty thorps, a little town,
  And half a hundred bridges. 30

Till last by Philip's farm I flow
  To join the brimming river,
For men may come and men may go,
  But I go on for ever.

'Poor lad, he died at Florence, quite worn out, 35
Travelling to Naples. There is Darnley bridge,
It has more ivy; there the river; and there
Stands Philip's farm where brook and river meet.

I chatter over stony ways,
  In little sharps and trebles, 40
I bubble into eddying bays,
  I babble on the pebbles.

With many a curve my banks I fret
  By many a field and fallow,
And many a fairy foreland set 45
  With willow-weed and mallow.

I chatter, chatter, as I flow
  To join the brimming river,
For men may come and men may go,
  But I go on for ever. 50

'But Philip chatter'd more than brook or bird;
Old Philip; all about the fields you caught
His weary daylong chirping, like the dry
High-elbow'd grigs that leap in summer grass.

I wind about, and in and out, 55
  With here a blossom sailing,
And here and there a lusty trout,
  And here and there a grayling,

29 *thorps* villages
54 *grigs* grasshoppers, crickets

And here and there a foamy flake
Upon me, as I travel 60
With many a silvery waterbreak
Above the golden gravel,

And draw them all along, and flow
To join the brimming river,
For men may come and men may go, 65
But I go on for ever.

'O darling Katie Willows, his one child!
A maiden of our century, yet most meek;
A daughter of our meadows, yet not coarse;
Straight, but as lissome as a hazel wand; 70
Her eyes a bashful azure, and her hair
In gloss and hue the chestnut, when the shell
Divides threefold to show the fruit within.

'Sweet Katie, once I did her a good turn,
Her and her far-off cousin and betrothed, 75
James Willows, of one name and heart with her.
For here I came, twenty years back—the week
Before I parted with poor Edmund; crost
By that old bridge which, half in ruins then,
Still makes a hoary eyebrow for the gleam 80
Beyond it, where the waters marry—crost,
Whistling a random bar of Bonny Doon,
And push'd at Philip's garden-gate. The gate,
Half-parted from a weak and scolding hinge,
Stuck; and he clamour'd from a casement, "Run" 85
To Katie somewhere in the walks below,
"Run, Katie!" Katie never ran: she moved
To meet me, winding under woodbine bowers,
A little flutter'd, with her eyelids down,
Fresh apple-blossom, blushing for a boon. 90

90 *blushing for a boon* embarrassed at asking a favour

'What was it? less of sentiment than sense
Had Katie; not illiterate; nor of those
Who dabbling in the fount of fictive tears,
And nursed by mealy-mouth'd philanthropies,
Divorce the Feeling from her mate the Deed. 95

'She told me. She and James had quarrell'd. Why?
What cause of quarrel? None, she said, no cause;
James had no cause: but when I prest the cause,
I learnt that James had flickering jealousies
Which anger'd her. Who anger'd James? I said. 100
But Katie snatch'd her eyes at once from mine,
And sketching with her slender pointed foot
Some figure like a wizard pentagram
On garden gravel, let my query pass
Unclaim'd, in flushing silence, till I ask'd 105
If James were coming. "Coming every day,"
She answer'd, "ever longing to explain,
But evermore her father came across
With some long-winded tale, and broke him short;
And James departed vext with him and her." 110
How could I help her? "Would I—was it wrong?"
(Claspt hands and that petitionary grace
Of sweet seventeen subdued me ere she spoke)
"O would I take her father for one hour,
For one half-hour, and let him talk to me!" 115
And even while she spoke, I saw where James
Made toward us, like a wader in the surf,
Beyond the brook, waist-deep in meadow-sweet.

92 *fictive* fictitious; artificial

94–5 she was not one of those who, brought up on namby-pamby ideas of 'charity', feel sympathy for others but *do* nothing (or alternatively *do* 'good works' without any genuine feeling behind them)

103 *pentagram* or pentacle. The 5-pointed star of magicians

'O Katie, what I suffer'd for your sake!
For in I went, and call'd old Philip out — 120
To show the farm: full willingly he rose:
He led me thro' the short sweet-smelling lanes
Of his wheat-suburb, babbling as he went.
He praised his land, his horses, his machines;
He praised his ploughs, his cows, his hogs, his dogs; — 125
He praised his hens, his geese, his guinea-hens;
His pigeons, who in session on their roofs
Approved him, bowing at their own deserts:
Then from the plaintive mother's teat he took
Her blind and shuddering puppies, naming each, — 130
And naming those, his friends, for whom they were:
Then crost the common into Darnley chase
To show Sir Arthur's deer. In copse and fern
Twinkled the innumerable ear and tail.

Then, seated on a serpent-rooted beech, — 135
He pointed out a pasturing colt, and said:
"That was the four-year-old I sold the Squire."
And there he told a long long-winded tale
Of how the Squire had seen the colt at grass,
And how it was the thing his daughter wish'd, — 140
And how he sent the bailiff to the farm
To learn the price, and what the price he ask'd,
And how the bailiff swore that he was mad,
But he stood firm; and so the matter hung;
He gave them line: and five days after that — 145

123 *wheat-suburb* wheat-fields lying round his farm like the suburbs of a town

128 *bowing at their own deserts* a masterly phrase. It suggests exactly the way in which pigeons appear both to compliment themselves and at the same time to acknowledge the compliment

133 *Sir Arthur* the Squire, no doubt

He met the bailiff at the Golden Fleece,
Who then and there had offer'd something more,
But he stood firm; and so the matter hung;
He knew the man; the colt would fetch its price;
He gave them line: and how by chance at last 150
(It might be May or April, he forgot,
The last of April or the first of May)
He found the bailiff riding by the farm,
And, talking from the point, he drew him in,
And there he mellow'd all his heart with ale, 155
Until they closed a bargain, hand in hand.

'Then, while I breathed in sight of haven, he,
Poor fellow, could he help it? recommenced,
And ran thro' all the coltish chronicle,
Wild Will, Black Bess, Tantivy, Tallyho, 160
Reform, White Rose, Bellerophon, the Jilt,
Arbaces, and Phenomenon, and the rest,
Till, not to die a listener, I arose,
And with me Philip, talking still; and so
We turn'd our foreheads from the falling sun, 165
And following our own shadows thrice as long
As when they follow'd us from Philip's door,
Arrived, and found the sun of sweet content
Re-risen in Katie's eyes, and all things well.

I steal by lawns and grassy plots, 170
I slide by hazel covers;
I move the sweet forget-me-nots
That grow for happy lovers.

157 *in sight of haven* of what haven?
161–2 *Bellerophon . . . Arbaces* mythical or historical figures. The name Bellerophon would be familiar at the time since the ship on which Napoleon surrendered in 1810 was named after him.

I slip, I slide, I gloom, I glance,
Among my skimming swallows; 175
I make the netted sunbeam dance
Against my sandy shallows.

I murmur under moon and stars
In brambly wildernesses;
I linger by my shingly bars; 180
I loiter round my cresses;

And out again I curve and flow
To join the brimming river,
For men may come and men may go,
But I go on for ever. 185

Yes, men may come and go; and these are gone,
All gone. My dearest brother, Edmund, sleeps,
Not by the well-known stream and rustic spire,
But unfamiliar Arno, and the dome
Of Brunelleschi; sleeps in peace: and he, 190
Poor Philip, of all his lavish waste of words
Remains the lean P. W. on his tomb:
I scraped the lichen from it: Katie walks
By the long wash of Australasian seas
Far off, and holds her head to other stars, 195
And breathes in April-autumns. All are gone.'

So Lawrence Aylmer, seated on a stile
In the long hedge, and rolling in his mind
Old waifs of rhyme, and bowing o'er the brook
A tonsured head in middle age forlorn, 200
Mused, and was mute. On a sudden a low breath
Of tender air made tremble in the hedge

189 *Arno* the river on which Florence stands. Brunelleschi's dome is on the Church of Santa Maria del Fiore (15th century)

The fragile bindweed-bells and briony rings;
And he look'd up. There stood a maiden near,
Waiting to pass. In much amaze he stared 205
On eyes a bashful azure, and on hair
In gloss and hue the chestnut, when the shell
Divides threefold to show the fruit within:
Then, wondering, ask'd her 'Are you from the farm?'
'Yes' answer'd she. 'Pray stay a little: pardon me; 210
What do they call you?' 'Katie.' 'That were strange.
What surname?' 'Willows.' 'No!' 'That is my name.'
'Indeed!' and here he look'd so self-perplext,
That Katie laugh'd, and laughing blush'd, till he
Laugh'd also, but as one before he wakes, 215
Who feels a glimmering strangeness in his dream.
Then looking at her; 'Too happy, fresh and fair,
Too fresh and fair in our sad world's best bloom,
To be the ghost of one who bore your name
About these meadows, twenty years ago.' 220

'Have you not heard?' said Katie, 'we came back.
We bought the farm we tenanted before.
Am I so like her? so they said on board.
Sir, if you knew her in her English days,
My mother, as it seems you did, the days 225
That most she loves to talk of, come with me.
My brother James is in the harvest-field:
But she—you will be welcome—O, come in!'

203 *bindweed-bells* convolvulus flowers
briony rings the clusters of flowers of wild bryony
206–8 Tennyson repeats the simile of ll. 71–3, not because he is proud of it (although he might well be), but to emphasise the likeness between this girl's hair and her mother's

SONGS FROM *THE PRINCESS*

I

As thro' the land at eve we went,
  And pluck'd the ripen'd ears,
We fell out, my wife and I,
O we fell out I know not why,
  And kiss'd again with tears. 5
And blessings on the falling out
  That all the more endears,
When we fall out with those we love
  And kiss again with tears!
For when we came where lies the child 10
  We lost in other years,
There above the little grave,
O there above the little grave,
  We kiss'd again with tears.

II

Sweet and low, sweet and low, 15
  Wind of the western sea,
Low, low, breathe and blow,
  Wind of the western sea!
Over the rolling waters go,
Come from the dying moon, and blow, 20
  Blow him again to me;
While my little one, while my pretty one, sleeps.

Sleep and rest, sleep and rest,
  Father will come to thee soon:
Rest, rest, on mother's breast, 25
  Father will come to thee soon:
Father will come to his babe in the nest,
Silver sails all out of the west
  Under the silver moon:
Sleep, my little one, sleep, my pretty one, sleep. 30

III

The splendour falls on castle walls
And snowy summits old in story:
The long light shakes across the lakes,
And the wild cataract leaps in glory.
Blow, bugle, blow, set the wild echoes flying, 35
Blow, bugle; answer, echoes, dying, dying, dying.

O hark, O hear! how thin and clear,
And thinner, clearer, farther going!
O sweet and far from cliff and scar
The horns of Elfland faintly blowing! 40
Blow, let us hear the purple glens replying:
Blow, bugle; answer, echoes, dying, dying, dying.

O love, they die in yon rich sky,
They faint on hill or field or river:
Our echoes roll from soul to soul, 45
And grow for ever and for ever.
Blow, bugle, blow, set the wild echoes flying,
And answer, echoes, answer, dying, dying, dying.

IV

'Tears, idle tears, I know not what they mean,
Tears from the depth of some divine despair 50
Rise in the heart, and gather to the eyes,
In looking on the happy Autumn-fields,
And thinking of the days that are no more.

'Fresh as the first beam glittering on a sail,
That brings our friends up from the underworld, 55
Sad as the last which reddens over one
That sinks with all we love below the verge;
So sad, so fresh, the days that are no more.

'Ah, sad and strange as in dark summer dawns
The earliest pipe of half-awaken'd birds   60
To dying ears, when unto dying eyes
The casement slowly grows a glimmering square;
So sad, so strange, the days that are no more.

'Dear as remember'd kisses after death,
And sweet as those by hopeless fancy feign'd   65
On lips that are for others; deep as love,
Deep as first love, and wild with all regret;
O Death in Life, the days that are no more.'

V

Home they brought her warrior dead:
She nor swoon'd, nor utter'd cry: 70
All her maidens, watching, said,
'She must weep or she will die.'

Then they praised him, soft and low,
Call'd him worthy to be loved,
Truest friend and noblest foe;   75
Yet she neither spoke nor moved.

Stole a maiden from her place,
Lightly to the warrior stept,
Took the face-cloth from the face;
Yet she neither moved nor wept.   80

Rose a nurse of ninety years,
Set his child upon her knee—
Like summer tempest came her tears—
'Sweet my child, I live for thee.'

VI

Ask me no more: the moon may draw the sea; 85
The cloud may stoop from heaven and take the shape
With fold to fold, of mountain or of cape;
But O too fond, when have I answer'd thee?
Ask me no more.

Ask me no more: what answer should I give? 90
I love not hollow cheek or faded eye:
Yet, O my friend, I will not have thee die!
Ask me no more, lest I should bid thee live;
Ask me no more.

Ask me no more: thy fate and mine are seal'd: 95
I strove against the stream and all in vain:
Let the great river take me to the main:
No more, dear love, for at a touch I yield;
Ask me no more.

VII

'Now sleeps the crimson petal, now the white; 100
Nor waves the cypress in the palace walk;
Nor winks the gold fin in the porphyry font:
The fire-fly wakens: waken thou with me.

Now droops the milkwhite peacock like a ghost,
And like a ghost she glimmers on to me. 105

Now lies the Earth all Danaë to the stars,
And all thy heart lies open unto me.

100 note that this lyric, like IV, is in blank verse
102 *porphyry* a hard, highly polished stone, usually red
104 *milkwhite* not the adjective one first thinks of in connection with the peacock. There is, however, a white variety
106 *all Danaë to the stars* Danaë was a princess who was 'visited' by Zeus in a shower of gold. Tennyson likens the stars to a shower of gold around Danaë, the earth

Now slides the silent meteor on, and leaves
A shining furrow, as thy thoughts in me.

Now folds the lily all her sweetness up, 110
And slips into the bosom of the lake:
So fold thyself, my dearest, thou, and slip
Into my bosom and be lost in me.'

VIII

'Come down, O maid, from yonder mountain height:
What pleasure lives in height (the shepherd sang) 115
In height and cold, the splendour of the hills?
But cease to move so near the Heavens, and cease
To glide a sunbeam by the blasted Pine,
To sit a star upon the sparkling spire:
And come, for Love is of the valley, come 120
For Love is of the valley, come thou down
And find him; by the happy threshold he,
Or hand in hand with Plenty in the maize,
Or red with spirted purple of the vats,
Or foxlike in the vine; nor cares to walk 125
With Death and Morning on the silver horns,
Nor wilt thou snare him in the white ravine,
Nor find him dropt upon the firths of ice,
That huddling slant in furrow-cloven falls
To roll the torrent out of dusky doors: 130
But follow; let the torrent dance thee down
To find him in the valley; let the wild
Lean-headed Eagles yelp alone, and leave
The monstrous ledges there to slope, and spill

118 *a sunbeam* 119 *a star* these nouns would normally be placed between commas—'to glide, a sunbeam, by . . . ,' 'to sit, a star, upon . . .'
122 *him . . . he . . .* the loved one
125 *nor cares* nor does he care

Their thousand wreaths of dangling water-smoke, 135
That like a broken purpose waste in air:
So waste not thou; but come; for all the vales
Await thee; azure pillars of the hearth
Arise to thee; the children call, and I
Thy shepherd pipe, and sweet is every sound, 140
Sweeter thy voice, but every sound is sweet;
Myriads of rivulets hurrying thro' the lawn,
The moan of doves in immemorial elms,
And murmuring of innumerable bees.'

Ode on the Death of the Duke of Wellington

PUBLISHED IN 1852

I

BURY the Great Duke
With an empire's lamentation,
Let us bury the Great Duke
To the noise of the mourning of a mighty nation,
Mourning when their leaders fall, 5
Warriors carry the warrior's pall,
And sorrow darkens hamlet and hall.

II

Where shall we lay the man whom we deplore?
Here, in streaming London's central roar.
Let the sound of those he wrought for, 10
And the feet of those he fought for,
Echo round his bones for evermore.

143 *immemorial* old, beyond memory
8 *deplore* this word has obviously changed its meaning since 1852

III

Lead out the pageant: sad and slow,
As fits an universal woe,
Let the long long procession go,
And let the sorrowing crowd about it grow,
And let the mournful martial music blow;
The last great Englishman is low.

IV

Mourn, for to us he seems the last,
Remembering all his greatness in the Past.
No more in soldier fashion will he greet
With lifted hand the gazer in the street.
O friends, our chief state-oracle is mute:
Mourn for the man of long-enduring blood,
The statesman-warrior, moderate, resolute,
Whole in himself, a common good.
Mourn for the man of amplest influence,
Yet clearest of ambitious crime,
Our greatest yet with least pretence,
Great in council and great in war,
Foremost captain of his time,
Rich in saving common-sense,
And, as the greatest only are,
In his simplicity sublime.
O good gray head which all men knew,
O voice from which their omens all men drew,
O iron nerve to true occasion true,
O fall'n at length that tower of strength
Which stood four-square to all the winds that blew!

30 *Great in council* few would endorse this view of Wellington as a statesman. Tennyson ignores Wellington's mistakes as Prime Minister unless his l. 32, 'Rich in saving common-sense' means more than it says

Such was he whom we deplore. 40
The long self-sacrifice of life is o'er.
The great World-victor's victor will be seen no more.

V

All is over and done:
Render thanks to the Giver,
England, for thy son. 45
Let the bell be toll'd.
Render thanks to the Giver,
And render him to the mould.
Under the cross of gold
That shines over city and river, 50
There he shall rest for ever
Among the wise and the bold.
Let the bell be toll'd:
And a reverent people behold
The towering car, the sable steeds: 55
Bright let it be with its blazon'd deeds,
Dark in its funeral fold.
Let the bell be toll'd:
And a deeper knell in the heart be knoll'd;
And the sound of the sorrowing anthem roll'd 60
Thro' the dome of the golden cross;
And the volleying cannon thunder his loss;
He knew their voices of old.
For many a time in many a clime
His captain's-ear has heard them boom 65
Bellowing victory, bellowing doom:

42 who was the great 'World-victor'?
55 *car* the funeral carriage
56 *blazon'd deeds* battle-honours embroidered on the pall (the *funeral fold* of l. 57)

When he with those deep voices wrought,
Guarding realms and kings from shame;
With those deep voices our dead captain taught
The tyrant, and asserts his claim 70
In that dread sound to the great name,
Which he has worn so pure of blame,
In praise and in dispraise the same,
A man of well-attemper'd frame.
O civic muse, to such a name, 75
To such a name for ages long,
To such a name,
Preserve a broad approach to fame,
And ever-echoing avenues of song.

VI

Who is he that cometh, like an honour'd guest, 80
With banner and with music, with soldier and with
priest,
With a nation weeping, and breaking on my rest?
Mighty Seaman, this is he
Was great by land as thou by sea.
Thine island loves thee well, thou famous man, 85
The greatest sailor since our world began.
Now, to the roll of muffled drums,
To thee the greatest soldier comes;
For this is he
Was great by land as thou by sea; 90
His foes were thine; he kept us free;
O give him welcome, this is he
Worthy of our gorgeous rites,
And worthy to be laid by thee;

74 *attemper'd* tempered, as steel is tempered
80–2 Nelson asks from his tomb who this newcomer may be

For this is England's greatest son, 95
He that gain'd a hundred fights,
Nor ever lost an English gun;
This is he that far away
Against the myriads of Assaye
Clash'd with his fiery few and won; 100
And underneath another sun,
Warring on a later day,
Round affrighted Lisbon drew
The treble works, the vast designs
Of his labour'd rampart-lines, 105
Where he greatly stood at bay,
Whence he issued forth anew,
And ever great and greater grew,
Beating from the wasted vines
Back to France her banded swarms, 110
Back to France with countless blows,
Till o'er the hills her eagles flew
Beyond the Pyrenean pines,
Follow'd up in valley and glen
With blare of bugle, clamour of men, 115
Roll of cannon and clash of arms,
And England pouring on her foes.
Such a war had such a close.
Again their ravening eagle rose
In anger, wheel'd on Europe-shadowing wings, 120
And barking for the thrones of kings;

99 *Assaye* a battle in India (1803) won by Sir Arthur Wellesley (as he then was) against heavy odds

104–5 *The treble works* the famous Lines of Torres Vedras. In 1810, Wellesley (as he still was) withdrew his armies behind three skilfully-placed and cleverly engineered lines of defence across the peninsula on which Lisbon stands. Here he was impregnable and able to gather strength for the 1812 offensive described in ll. 107–17

121 *barking* as good a word as any for the cry of an eagle

Till one that sought but Duty's iron crown
On that loud sabbath shook the spoiler down;
A day of onsets of despair!
Dash'd on every rocky square 125
Their surging charges foam'd themselves away;
Last, the Prussian trumpet blew;
Thro' the long-tormented air
Heaven flash'd a sudden jubilant ray,
And down we swept and charged and overthrew. 130
So great a soldier taught us there,
What long-enduring hearts could do
In that world-earthquake, Waterloo!
Mighty Seaman, tender and true,
And pure as he from taint of craven guile, 135
O saviour of the silver-coasted isle,
O shaker of the Baltic and the Nile,
If aught of things that here befall
Touch a spirit among things divine,
If love of country move thee here at all, 140
Be glad, because his bones are laid by thine!
And thro' the centuries let a people's voice
In full acclaim,
A people's voice,
The proof and echo of all human fame, 145
A people's voice, when they rejoice
At civic revel and pomp and game,
Attest their great commander's claim
With honour, honour, honour, honour to him,
Eternal honour to his name. 150

123 *On that loud sabbath* Waterloo was fought on Sunday, June 18th

127 *the Prussian trumpet* the arrival of the Prussian troops under Blücher finally turned the scale

VII

A people's voice! we are a people yet.
Tho' all men else their nobler dreams forget,
Confused by brainless mobs and lawless Powers;
Thank Him who isled us here, and roughly set
His Briton in blown seas and storming showers, 155
We have a voice, with which to pay the debt
Of boundless love and reverence and regret
To those great men who fought, and kept it ours.
And keep it ours, O God, from brute control;
O Statesmen, guard us, guard the eye, the soul 160
Of Europe, keep our noble England whole,
And save the one true seed of freedom sown
Betwixt a people and their ancient throne,
That sober freedom out of which there springs
Our loyal passion for our temperate kings; 165
For, saving that, ye help to save mankind
Till public wrong be crumbled into dust,
And drill the raw world for the march of mind,
Till crowds at length be sane and crowns be just.
But wink no more in slothful overtrust. 170
Remember him who led your hosts;
He bad you guard the sacred coasts.
Your cannons moulder on the seaward wall;
His voice is silent in your council-hall
For ever; and whatever tempests lour 175
For ever silent; even if they broke
In thunder, silent; yet remember all

151–91 see *Notes*
155 *Briton* more correctly, Britain
170 *wink* close the eye, fail to see
slothful overtrust Tennyson laments the state of England's defences (l. 173) and attributes her unpreparedness to a combination of 'sloth' and over-confidence

He spoke among you, and the Man who spoke;
Who never sold the truth to serve the hour,
Nor palter'd with Eternal God for power, 180
Who let the turbid streams of rumour flow
Thro' either babbling world of high and low;
Whose life was work, whose language rife
With rugged maxims hewn from life;
Who never spoke against a foe; 185
Whose eighty winters freeze with one rebuke
All great self-seekers trampling on the right:
Truth-teller was our England's Alfred named;
Truth-lover was our English Duke;
Whatever record leap to light 190
He never shall be shamed.

VIII

Lo, the leader in these glorious wars
Now to glorious burial slowly borne,
Follow'd by the brave of other lands,
He, on whom from both her open hands 195
Lavish Honour shower'd all her stars,
And affluent Fortune emptied all her horn.
Yea, let all good things await
Him who cares not to be great,
But as he saves or serves the state. 200
Not once or twice in our rough island-story,
The path of duty was the way to glory:
He that walks it, only thirsting

180 *palter'd* played fast and loose
203–8 he who treads the path of duty, thirsting only for the right and suppressing all self-interest, will find before the end of his days that what seemed to him stubborn thistles will burst into gorgeous regal flowers (*glossy purples*) far superior even to the loveliest roses. A less successful metaphor than its companion (ll. 211–17)

For the right, and learns to deaden
Love of self, before his journey closes, 205
He shall find the stubborn thistle bursting
Into glossy purples, which outredden
All voluptuous garden-roses.
Not once or twice in our fair island-story,
The path of duty was the way to glory: 210
He, that ever following her commands,
On with toil of heart and knees and hands,
Thro' the long gorge to the far light has won
His path upward, and prevail'd,
Shall find the toppling crags of Duty scaled 215
Are close upon the shining table-lands
To which our God Himself is moon and sun.
Such was he: his work is done.
But while the races of mankind endure,
Let his great example stand 220
Colossal, seen of every land,
And keep the soldier firm, the statesman pure:
Till in all lands and thro' all human story
The path of duty be the way to glory:
And let the land whose hearths he saved from shame 225
For many and many an age proclaim
At civic revel and pomp and game,
And when the long-illumined cities flame,
Their ever-loyal iron leader's fame,
With honour, honour, honour, honour to him, 230
Eternal honour to his name.

IX

Peace, his triumph will be sung
By some yet unmoulded tongue

215 *scaled* once they are scaled

Far on in summers that we shall not see:
Peace, it is a day of pain 235
For one about whose patriarchal knee
Late the little children clung:
O peace, it is a day of pain
For one, upon whose hand and heart and brain
Once the weight and fate of Europe hung. 240
Ours the pain, be his the gain!
More than is of man's degree
Must be with us, watching here
At this, our great solemnity.
Whom we see not we revere; 245
We revere, and we refrain
From talk of battles loud and vain,
And brawling memories all too free
For such a wise humility
As befits a solemn fane: 250
We revere, and while we hear
The tides of Music's golden sea
Setting toward eternity,
Uplifted high in heart and hope are we,
Until we doubt not that for one so true 255
There must be other nobler work to do
Than when he fought at Waterloo,
And Victor he must ever be.
For tho' the Giant Ages heave the hill
And break the shore, and evermore 260
Make and break, and work their will;
Tho' world on world in myriad myriads roll
Round us, each with different powers,
And other forms of life than ours,
What know we greater than the soul? 265

259–64 a reflection of Tennyson's interest in geology and astronomy

On God and Godlike men we build our trust.
Hush, the Dead March wails in the people's ears:
The dark crowd moves, and there are sobs and tears:
The black earth yawns: the mortal disappears;
Ashes to ashes, dust to dust; 270
He is gone who seem'd so great.—
Gone; but nothing can bereave him
Of the force he made his own
Being here, and we believe him
Something far advanced in State, 275
And that he wears a truer crown
Than any wreath that man can weave him.
Speak no more of his renown,
Lay your earthly fancies down,
And in the vast cathedral leave him, 280
God accept him, Christ receive him.

1852.

The Charge of the Light Brigade

I

HALF a league, half a league,
Half a league onward,
All in the valley of Death
Rode the six hundred.
'Forward, the Light Brigade! 5
Charge for the guns!' he said:
Into the valley of Death
Rode the six hundred.

6 *he* see *Notes*

II

'Forward, the Light Brigade!'
Was there a man dismay'd?
Not tho' the soldier knew
    Some one had blunder'd:
Their's not to make reply,
Their's not to reason why,
Their's but to do and die:
Into the valley of Death
    Rode the six hundred.

III

Cannon to right of them,
Cannon to left of them,
Cannon in front of them
    Volley'd and thunder'd;
Storm'd at with shot and shell,
Boldly they rode and well,
Into the jaws of Death,
Into the mouth of Hell
    Rode the six hundred.

IV

Flash'd all their sabres bare,
Flash'd as they turn'd in air
Sabring the gunners there,
Charging an army, while
    All the world wonder'd:
Plunged in the battery-smoke
Right thro' the line they broke;
Cossack and Russian
Reel'd from the sabre-stroke

13, 14, 15 *Their's* incorrect. It should be *Theirs*

Shatter'd and sunder'd.
Then they rode back, but not
Not the six hundred.

V

Cannon to right of them,
Cannon to left of them, 40
Cannon behind them
Volley'd and thunder'd;
Storm'd at with shot and shell,
While horse and hero fell,
They that had fought so well 45
Came thro' the jaws of Death,
Back from the mouth of Hell,
All that was left of them,
Left of six hundred.

VI

When can their glory fade? 50
O the wild charge they made!
All the world wonder'd.
Honour the charge they made!
Honour the Light Brigade,
Noble six hundred! 55

Flower in the Crannied Wall

FLOWER in the crannied wall,
I pluck you out of the crannies,
I hold you here, root and all, in my hand,
Little flower—but *if* I could understand
What you are, root and all, and all in all,
I should know what God and man is.

FROM

In Memoriam A. H. H.

OBIIT MDCCCXXXIII

STRONG Son of God, immortal Love,
  Whom we, that have not seen thy face,
  By faith, and faith alone, embrace,
Believing where we cannot prove;

Thine are these orbs of light and shade; 5
  Thou madest Life in man and brute;
  Thou madest Death; and lo, thy foot
Is on the skull which thou hast made.

Thou wilt not leave us in the dust:
  Thou madest man, he knows not why, 10
  He thinks he was not made to die;
And thou hast made him: thou art just.

Thou seemest human and divine,
  The highest, holiest manhood, thou:
  Our wills are ours, we know not how; 15
Our wills are ours, to make them thine.

Our little systems have their day;
  They have their day and cease to be:
  They are but broken lights of thee,
And thou, O Lord, art more than they. 20

5 *orbs of light and shade* the sun and the moon
11 man believes that death is not the end of all things
17 *Our little systems* (in this context) our various Churches and sects

We have but faith: we cannot know;
For knowledge is of things we see;
And yet we trust it comes from thee,
A beam in darkness: let it grow.

Let knowledge grow from more to more, 25
But more of reverence in us dwell;
That mind and soul, according well,
May make one music as before,

But vaster. We are fools and slight;
We mock thee when we do not fear: 30
But help thy foolish ones to bear;
Help thy vain worlds to bear thy light.

Forgive what seem'd my sin in me;
What seem'd my worth since I began;
For merit lives from man to man, 35
And not from man, O Lord, to thee.

Forgive my grief for one removed,
Thy creature, whom I found so fair.
I trust he lives in thee, and there
I find him worthier to be loved. 40

24 *A beam in darkness* a light to lighten our ignorance
28 *as before* as in the old days, when there was 'one music', one undivided Christian Church
29 *slight* insignificant, weak
30 those men who do not fear God, 'mock' him
35–6 human virtues ('merit') are measured by comparison between man and man, not between man and God

Forgive these wild and wandering cries,
  Confusions of a wasted youth;
  Forgive them where they fail in truth,
And in thy wisdom make me wise.

1849.

I

I HELD it truth, with him who sings 45
  To one clear harp in divers tones,
  That men may rise on stepping-stones
Of their dead selves to higher things.

But who shall so forecast the years
  And find in loss a gain to match? 50
  Or reach a hand thro' time to catch
The far-off interest of tears?

Let Love clasp Grief lest both be drown'd,
  Let darkness keep her raven gloss:
  Ah, sweeter to be drunk with loss, 55
To dance with death, to beat the ground,

Than that the victor Hours should scorn
  The long result of love, and boast,
  'Behold the man that loved and lost,
But all he was is overworn.' 60

42 *wasted youth* Tennyson seems here to reproach himself for 'wasting' his youth in grief for his friend

45 *him* Goethe, the German poet, who wrote in various literary forms ('in divers tones')—poetry, drama, criticism, etc—but always on a lofty moral note ('to one clear harp')

52 the ultimate ('far-off') rewards ('interest') of grief ('tears'); i.e., the good that man learns, in the end, through sorrow

56 *to beat the ground* suggestive of some savage dance of mourning

57 *victor Hours* triumphant Time

60 *overworn* worn out, finished

XI

Calm is the morn without a sound,
Calm as to suit a calmer grief,
And only thro' the faded leaf
The chestnut pattering to the ground:

Calm and deep peace on this high wold, 65
And on these dews that drench the furze,
And all the silvery gossamers
That twinkle into green and gold:

Calm and still light on yon great plain
That sweeps with all its autumn bowers, 70
And crowded farms and lessening towers,
To mingle with the bounding main:

Calm and deep peace in this wide air,
These leaves that redden to the fall;
And in my heart, if calm at all, 75
If any calm, a calm despair:

Calm on the seas, and silver sleep,
And waves that sway themselves in rest,
And dead calm in that noble breast
Which heaves but with the heaving deep. 80

62 *a calmer grief* calmer than the poet's. The morning is calm enough to suit a grief that was calmer than his grief: it was *too* calm for him

67 *gossamers* the delicate spiders' webs seen on the grass on a fine autumn morning

71 *lessening towers* a closely-packed image. Tennyson refers to the church towers visible from the 'high wold'. The further off they are, the smaller they seem

77–80 Tennyson, in Lincolnshire, compares his calm with that in the heart of the dead Hallam ('in that noble breast') on the ship which is bringing his body home to England

XIX

The Danube to the Severn gave
The darken'd heart that beat no more;
They laid him by the pleasant shore,
And in the hearing of the wave.

There twice a day the Severn fills; 85
The salt sea-water passes by,
And hushes half the babbling Wye,
And makes a silence in the hills.

The Wye is hush'd nor moved along,
And hush'd my deepest grief of all, 90
When fill'd with tears that cannot fall,
I brim with sorrow drowning song.

The tide flows down, the wave again
Is vocal in its wooded walls;
My deeper anguish also falls, 95
And I can speak a little then.

XXVIII

The time draws near the birth of Christ:
The moon is hid; the night is still;
The Christmas bells from hill to hill
Answer each other in the mist. 100

81 *The Danube* Hallam died in Vienna, on the Danube
the Severn he was buried at Clevedon, on the Severn estuary
85–9 a reference to the 'bore' or tidal wave which twice a day 'fills' the Severn and even affects its tributary, the Wye, for half its course. When the tide is in, the 'babbling' Wye runs silently
93–6 just as the river becomes 'vocal' as the tide runs out, so the poet's sorrow can find words when his grief ebbs a little
97 the first Christmas (1834) after Hallam's burial at Clevedon

Four voices of four hamlets round,
From far and near, on mead and moor,
Swell out and fail, as if a door
Were shut between me and the sound:

Each voice four changes on the wind, 105
That now dilate, and now decrease,
Peace and goodwill, goodwill and peace,
Peace and goodwill, to all mankind.

This year I slept and woke with pain,
I almost wish'd no more to wake, 110
And that my hold on life would break
Before I heard those bells again:

But they my troubled spirit rule,
For they controll'd me when a boy;
They bring me sorrow touch'd with joy, 115
The merry merry bells of Yule.

XXX

With trembling fingers did we weave
The holly round the Christmas hearth;
A rainy cloud possess'd the earth,
And sadly fell our Christmas-eve. 120

105 *four changes* possibly 'changes' in the bell-ringers' sense (the order in which the bells in a peal are rung). On the other hand Tennyson may have had in mind the phrase in ll. 107 and 108, 'Peace and goodwill', with each church bell ringing a different note for the four syllables

109 *This year I slept* he means that throughout the year he has been going to sleep, almost hoping he would not wake up, but waking 'with pain'. (See *Introduction*, p. 17)

117 *we* Christmas celebrations at Somersby, where Hallam had been a frequent and well-loved visitor, must have been a mockery for the whole family

At our old pastimes in the hall
    We gambol'd, making vain pretence
    Of gladness, with an awful sense
Of one mute Shadow watching all.

We paused: the winds were in the beech: 125
    We heard them sweep the winter land;
    And in a circle hand-in-hand
Sat silent, looking each at each.

Then echo-like our voices rang;
    We sung, tho' every eye was dim, 130
    A merry song we sang with him
Last year: impetuously we sang:

We ceased: a gentler feeling crept
    Upon us: surely rest is meet:
    'They rest,' we said, 'their sleep is sweet,' 135
And silence follow'd, and we wept.

Our voices took a higher range;
    Once more we sang: 'They do not die
    Nor lose their mortal sympathy,
Nor change to us, although they change; 140

'Rapt from the fickle and the frail
    With gather'd power, yet the same,

132 *Last year* not last Christmas, because Hallam died in September 1833. Presumably at some happy gathering some time in the year

141–4 A difficult stanza. The subject of the sentence appears to be 'the keen seraphic flame' (i.e. the spirit or soul of the dead) which, although snatched from the earthly body ('Rapt from the fickle and the frail'), is stronger yet still 'the same', and bridges the gap between this world and the next ('pierces . . . from orb to orb'); between the mystery of life and the mystery of death ('from veil to veil')

Pierces the keen seraphic flame
From orb to orb, from veil to veil.'

Rise, happy morn, rise, holy morn, 145
Draw forth the cheerful day from night:
O Father, touch the east, and light
The light that shone when Hope was born.

LIV

Oh yet we trust that somehow good
Will be the final goal of ill, 150
To pangs of nature, sins of will,
Defects of doubt, and taints of blood;

That nothing walks with aimless feet;
That not one life shall be destroy'd,
Or cast as rubbish to the void, 155
When God hath made the pile complete;

That not a worm is cloven in vain;
That not a moth with vain desire
Is shrivell'd in a fruitless fire,
Or but subserves another's gain. 160

Behold, we know not anything;
I can but trust that good shall fall
At last—far off—at last, to all,
And every winter change to spring.

151 *nature* human nature
sins of will deliberate or intentional sins
152 *Defects of doubt* errors arising from confusion between what is good and what is evil
taints of blood inherited sinfulness

So runs my dream: but what am I? 165
An infant crying in the night:
An infant crying for the light:
And with no language but a cry.

LXXXVI

Sweet after showers, ambrosial air,
That rollest from the gorgeous gloom 170
Of evening over brake and bloom
And meadow, slowly breathing bare

The round of space, and rapt below
Thro' all the dewy-tassell'd wood,
And shadowing down the horned flood 175
In ripples, fan my brows and blow

The fever from my cheek, and sigh
The full new life that feeds thy breath
Throughout my frame, till Doubt and Death,
Ill brethren, let the fancy fly 180

165–8 Tennyson has tried to comfort himself with the thought that 'somehow' good will come of ill; that there is a divine purpose in everything, even in the death of the smallest creature, such as a worm or a moth. After all, spring always comes after every winter. But then he calls this comforting thought a 'dream', and is left uncomforted like a child crying in the night (ignorance) for the light (divine wisdom)
169 *ambrosial air* Tennyson here addresses the air
171 *brake* fern, bracken
172 *breathing bare* blowing (the sky) clean
175 *horned flood* the river running between two tongues of land, as though it had horns. (Tennyson is presumably looking down on the scene from a height)
180 *let the fancy fly* let the imagination free to fly

From belt to belt of crimson seas
  On leagues of odour streaming far,
  To where in yonder orient star
A hundred spirits whisper 'Peace.'

CVI

Ring out, wild bells, to the wild sky, 185
  The flying cloud, the frosty light:
  The year is dying in the night;
Ring out, wild bells, and let him die.

Ring out the old, ring in the new,
  Ring, happy bells, across the snow: 190
  The year is going, let him go;
Ring out the false, ring in the true.

Ring out the grief that saps the mind,
  For those that here we see no more;
  Ring out the feud of rich and poor, 195
Ring in redress to all mankind.

Ring out a slowly dying cause,
  And ancient forms of party strife;
  Ring in the nobler modes of life,
With sweeter manners, purer laws. 200

Ring out the want, the care, the sin,
  The faithless coldness of the times;

182 *leagues of odour* a reference back to 'ambrosial' in l. 169—the fragrant air

183 *orient star* the star rising in the East. The whole section is a reference to the growth of 'new life' (l. 178), of new friendships ('orient star') which will drive away the clouds of sorrow and bring peace. Note that the 16 lines of LXXXVI make a single sentence

Ring out, ring out my mournful rhymes,
But ring the fuller minstrel in.

Ring out false pride in place and blood, 205
The civic slander and the spite;
Ring in the love of truth and right,
Ring in the common love of good.

Ring out old shapes of foul disease;
Ring out the narrowing lust of gold; 210
Ring out the thousand wars of old,
Ring in the thousand years of peace.

Ring in the valiant man and free,
The larger heart, the kindlier hand;
Ring out the darkness of the land, 215
Ring in the Christ that is to be.

CXV

Now fades the last long streak of snow,
Now burgeons every maze of quick
About the flowering squares, and thick
By ashen roots the violets blow. 220

Now rings the woodland loud and long,
The distance takes a lovelier hue,

203–4 it is difficult to judge the sincerity of these two lines, but apparently Tennyson meant that he had no preference for writing sad verses but would rather be composing in 'fuller', i.e., richer, more varied, strains

218 *burgeons* buds
maze of quick thicket (or hedge) of hawthorn

219 *flowering squares* either flower-beds, with spring flowers, or fields with wild flowers in bloom

220 *ashen roots* presumably the roots of ash-trees; but it could be the bare, grey, exposed roots of any trees

And drown'd in yonder living blue
The lark becomes a sightless song.

Now dance the lights on lawn and lea, 225
The flocks are whiter down the vale,
And milkier every milky sail
On winding stream or distant sea;

Where now the seamew pipes, or dives
In yonder greening gleam, and fly 230
The happy birds, that change their sky
To build and brood; that live their lives

From land to land; and in my breast
Spring wakens too; and my regret
Becomes an April violet, 235
And buds and blossoms like the rest.

IDYLLS OF THE KING

The Coming of Arthur

LEODOGRAN, the King of Cameliard,
Had one fair daughter, and none other child;
And she was fairest of all flesh on earth,
Guinevere, and in her his one delight.

224 *sightless* invisible
225 *dance the lights* the spring sunshine is reflected in pools from the melted snow
230–1 *fly / the happy birds* verb before subject—a poetic inversion
231 *that change their sky* birds migrate just before the mating season
233–6 the coming of spring re-awakens the poet's sorrow ('my regret') but this time with the promise of better, happier times to come

1 In Malory he is Leodegrance
Cameliard three syllables

For many a petty king ere Arthur came 5
Ruled in this isle, and ever waging war
Each upon other, wasted all the land;
And still from time to time the heathen host
Swarm'd overseas, and harried what was left.
And so there grew great tracts of wilderness, 10
Wherein the beast was ever more and more,
But man was less and less, till Arthur came.
For first Aurelius lived and fought and died,
And after him King Uther fought and died,
But either fail'd to make the kingdom one. 15
And after these King Arthur for a space,
And thro' the puissance of his Table Round,
Drew all their petty princedoms under him,
Their king and head, and made a realm, and reign'd.

And thus the land of Cameliard was waste, 20
Thick with wet woods, and many a beast therein,
And none or few to scare or chase the beast;
So that wild dog, and wolf and boar and bear
Came night and day, and rooted in the fields,
And wallow'd in the gardens of the King. 25
And ever and anon the wolf would steal
The children and devour, but now and then,
Her own brood lost or dead, lent her fierce teat
To human sucklings; and the children, housed
In her foul den, there at their meat would growl, 30
And mock their foster-mother on four feet,
Till, straighten'd, they grew up to wolf-like men,
Worse than the wolves. And King Leodogran
Groan'd for the Roman legions here again,

34 *Groan'd for the Roman legions*, etc. one of the few hints as to the date of the Arthurian era. See also ll. 502–13

And Cæsar's eagle: then his brother king, 35
Urien, assail'd him: last a heathen horde,
Reddening the sun with smoke and earth with blood,
And on the spike that split the mother's heart
Spitting the child, brake on him, till, amazed,
He knew not whither he should turn for aid. 40

But—for he heard of Arthur newly crown'd,
Tho' not without an uproar made by those
Who cried, 'He is not Uther's son'—the King
Sent to him, saying, 'Arise, and help us thou!
For here between the man and beast we die.' 45

And Arthur yet had done no deed of arms,
But heard the call, and came: and Guinevere
Stood by the castle walls to watch him pass;
But since he neither wore on helm or shield
The golden symbol of his kinglihood, 50
But rode a simple knight among his knights,
And many of these in richer arms than he,
She saw him not, or mark'd not, if she saw,
One among many, tho' his face was bare.
But Arthur, looking downward as he past, 55
Felt the light of her eyes into his life
Smite on the sudden, yet rode on, and pitch'd
His tents beside the forest. Then he drave
The heathen; after, slew the beast, and fell'd
The forest, letting in the sun, and made 60
Broad pathways for the hunter and the knight
And so return'd.

43 *He is not Uther's son* see ll. 67–73
55 *looking downward* why 'downward'?

For while he linger'd there,
A doubt that ever smoulder'd in the hearts
Of those great Lords and Barons of his realm
Flash'd forth and into war: for most of these, 65
Colleaguing with a score of petty kings,
Made head against him, crying, 'Who is he
That he should rule us? who hath proven him
King Uther's son? for lo! we look at him,
And find nor face nor bearing, limbs nor voice, 70
Are like to those of Uther whom we knew.
This is the son of Gorloïs, not the King;
This is the son of Anton, not the King.'

And Arthur, passing thence to battle, felt
Travail, and throes and agonies of the life, 75
Desiring to be join'd with Guinevere;
And thinking as he rode, 'Her father said
That there between the man and beast they die.
Shall I not lift her from this land of beasts
Up to my throne, and side by side with me? 80
What happiness to reign a lonely king,
Vext—O ye stars that shudder over me,
O earth that soundest hollow under me,
Vext with waste dreams? for saving I be join'd
To her that is the fairest under heaven, 85
I seem as nothing in the mighty world,
And cannot will my will, nor work my work

72 *Gorloïs* king of Cornwall. The scandal and gossip about Arthur's legitimacy was not unfounded. King Uther fell in love with Igraine, wife of Gorloïs, and with the help of Merlin's magic assumed the likeness of Gorloïs. Arthur was the result of this intrigue

73 *Anton* another king or princeling in Uther's court (see ll. 220–223)

75 *the life* of a soldier

81 *to reign* (would there be) in reigning

Wholly, nor make myself in mine own realm
Victor and lord. But were I join'd with her,
Then might we live together as one life, 90
And reigning with one will in everything
Have power on this dark land to lighten it,
And power on this dead world to make it live.'

Thereafter—as he speaks who tells the tale—
When Arthur reach'd a field-of-battle bright 95
With pitch'd pavilions of his foe, the world
Was all so clear about him, that he saw
The smallest rock far on the faintest hill,
And even in high day the morning star.
So when the King had set his banner broad, 100
At once from either side, with trumpet-blast,
And shouts, and clarions shrilling unto blood,
The long-lanced battle let their horses run.
And now the Barons and the kings prevail'd,
And now the King, as here and there that war 105
Went swaying; but the Powers who walk the world
Made lightnings and great thunders over him,
And dazed all eyes, till Arthur by main might,
And mightier of his hands with every blow,
And leading all his knighthood threw the kings 110
Carádos, Urien, Cradlemont of Wales,
Claudias, and Clariance of Northumberland,

96 *pavilions* tents
102 *clarions* high-pitched trumpets (hence 'shrilling')
103 *battle* army
111–15 these names are taken from Malory. Only Lot of Orkney is of importance in the Arthurian legends. He had married a sister of Arthur and their son was Mordred, or Modred. (See *Notes* to *Morte d'Arthur*.) Lot was also known as King of Norway, of which kingdom the Orkneys then formed part

The King Brandagoras of Latangor,
With Anguisant of Erin, Morganore,
And Lot of Orkney. Then, before a voice 115
As dreadful as the shout of one who sees
To one who sins, and deems himself alone
And all the world asleep, they swerved and brake
Flying, and Arthur call'd to stay the brands
That hack'd among the flyers, 'Ho! they yield!' 120
So like a painted battle the war stood
Silenced, the living quiet as the dead,
And in the heart of Arthur joy was lord.
He laugh'd upon his warrior whom he loved
And honour'd most. 'Thou dost not doubt me King, 125
So well thine arm hath wrought for me to-day.'
'Sir and my liege,' he cried, 'the fire of God
Descends upon thee in the battle-field:
I know thee for my King!' Whereat the two,
For each had warded either in the fight, 130
Sware on the field of death a deathless love.
And Arthur said, 'Man's word is God in man:
Let chance what will, I trust thee to the death.'

Then quickly from the foughten field he sent
Ulfius, and Brastias, and Bedivere, 135
His new-made knights, to King Leodogran,
Saying, 'If I in aught have served thee well,
Give me thy daughter Guinevere to wife.'

115 *a voice* a fine simile; is it in place here?
124–5 *his warrior . . . most* Lancelot, presumably. (Tennyson sometimes, as here, seems to be wilfully obscure, as though showing off to the ignorant people who had not read their Malory. But see l. 447)
125 *doubt me king* doubt that I am king
130 *warded* protected. Possibly each had saved the other's life

Whom when he heard, Leodogran in heart
Debating—'How should I that am a king, 140
However much he holp me at my need,
Give my one daughter saving to a king,
And a king's son?'—lifted his voice, and call'd
A hoary man, his chamberlain, to whom
He trusted all things, and of him required 145
His counsel: 'Knowest thou aught of Arthur's birth?'

Then spake the hoary chamberlain and said,
'Sir King, there be but two old men that know:
And each is twice as old as I; and one
Is Merlin, the wise man that ever served 150
King Uther thro' his magic art; and one
Is Merlin's master (so they call him) Bleys,
Who taught him magic; but the scholar ran
Before the master, and so far, that Bleys
Laid magic by, and sat him down, and wrote 155
All things and whatsoever Merlin did
In one great annal-book, where after-years
Will learn the secret of our Arthur's birth.'

To whom the King Leodogran replied,
'O friend, had I been holpen half as well 160
By this King Arthur as by thee to-day,
Then beast and man had had their share of me:
But summon here before us yet once more
Ulfius, and Brastias, and Bedivere.'

139 *Whom when he heard* and when he heard him. Even in a narrative poem about early Britain Tennyson uses Latin construction
141 *holp* obsolete past tense of help
144 *hoary* white-haired
150, 152 *Merlin . . . Bleys* see *Notes*
153–4 *the scholar ran / before the master* the pupil out-distanced his teacher

Then, when they came before him, the King said, 16
'I have seen the cuckoo chased by lesser fowl,
And reason in the chase: but wherefore now
Do these your lords stir up the heat of war,
Some calling Arthur born of Gorloïs,
Others of Anton? Tell me, ye yourselves, 17
Hold ye this Arthur for King Uther's son?'

And Ulfius and Brastias answer'd, 'Ay.'
Then Bedivere, the first of all his knights
Knighted by Arthur at his crowning, spake—
For bold in heart and act and word was he, 17
Whenever slander breathed against the King—

'Sir, there be many rumours on this head:
For there be those who hate him in their hearts,
Call him baseborn, and since his ways are sweet,
And theirs are bestial, hold him less than man: 18
And there be those who deem him more than man,
And dream he dropt from heaven; but my belief
In all this matter—so ye care to learn—
Sir, for ye know that in King Uther's time
The prince and warrior Gorloïs, he that held 18
Tintagil castle by the Cornish sea,
Was wedded with a winsome wife, Ygerne:
And daughters had she borne him,—one whereof,
Lot's wife, the Queen of Orkney, Bellicent,
Hath ever like a loyal sister cleaved 19
To Arthur,—but a son she had not borne.
And Uther cast upon her eyes of love:
But she, a stainless wife to Gorloïs,
So loathed the bright dishonour of his love,

167 *And reason in the chase* and D have seen) why

That Gorloïs and King Uther went to war: 195
And overthrown was Gorloïs and slain.
Then Uther in his wrath and heat besieged
Ygerne within Tintagil, where her men,
Seeing the mighty swarm about their walls,
Left her and fled, and Uther enter'd in, 200
And there was none to call to but himself.
So, compass'd by the power of the King,
Enforced she was to wed him in her tears,
And with a shameful swiftness: afterward,
Not many moons, King Uther died himself, 205
Moaning and wailing for an heir to rule
After him, lest the realm should go to wrack.
And that same night, the night of the new year,
By reason of the bitterness and grief
That vext his mother, all before his time 210
Was Arthur born, and all as soon as born
Deliver'd at a secret postern-gate
To Merlin, to be holden far apart
Until his hour should come; because the lords
Of that fierce day were as the lords of this, 215
Wild beasts, and surely would have torn the child
Piecemeal among them, had they known; for each
But sought to rule for his own self and hand,
And many hated Uther for the sake
Of Gorloïs. Wherefore Merlin took the child, 220
And gave him to Sir Anton, an old knight
And ancient friend of Uther; and his wife
Nursed the young prince, and rear'd him with her own;
And no man knew. And ever since the lords
Have foughten like wild beasts among themselves, 225

197–204 Tennyson, perhaps out of respect to Victorian morality, adopts a slightly different explanation of Arthur's birth and parenthood from Malory's version

So that the realm has gone to wrack: but now,
This year, when Merlin (for his hour had come)
Brought Arthur forth, and set him in the hall,
Proclaiming, "Here is Uther's heir, your king,"
A hundred voices cried, "Away with him! 230
No king of ours! a son of Gorloïs he,
Or else the child of Anton, and no king,
Or else baseborn." Yet Merlin thro' his craft,
And while the people clamour'd for a king,
Had Arthur crown'd; but after, the great lords 235
Banded, and so brake out in open war.'

Then while the King debated with himself
If Arthur were the child of shamefulness,
Or born the son of Gorloïs, after death,
Or Uther's son, and born before his time, 240
Or whether there were truth in anything
Said by these three, there came to Cameliard,
With Gawain and young Modred, her two sons,
Lot's wife, the Queen of Orkney, Bellicent;
Whom as he could, not as he would, the King 245
Made feast for, saying, as they sat at meat,

'A doubtful throne is ice on summer seas.
Ye come from Arthur's court. Victor his men
Report him! Yea, but ye—think ye this king—
So many those that hate him, and so strong, 250
So few his knights, however brave they be—
Hath body enow to hold his foemen down?'

227 *his hour* whose hour?

245 *as he could, not as he would* to the best of his ability, but not as he would have liked to (or perhaps unwillingly)

247 a throne which is not firmly and legitimately held is no safer than a lump of ice in warm water

'O King,' she cried, 'and I will tell thee: few,
Few, but all brave, all of one mind with him;
For I was near him when the savage yells 255
Of Uther's peerage died, and Arthur sat
Crown'd on the daïs, and his warriors cried,
"Be thou the king, and we will work thy will
Who love thee." Then the King in low deep tones,
And simple words of great authority, 260
Bound them by so strait vows to his own self,
That when they rose, knighted from kneeling, some
Were pale as at the passing of a ghost,
Some flush'd, and others dazed, as one who wakes
Half-blinded at the coming of a light. 265

'But when he spake and cheer'd his Table Round
With large, divine, and comfortable words,
Beyond my tongue to tell thee—I beheld
From eye to eye thro' all their Order flash
A momentary likeness of the King: 270
And ere it left their faces, thro' the cross
And those around it and the Crucified,
Down from the casement over Arthur, smote
Flame-colour, vert and azure, in three rays,
One falling upon each of three fair queens, 275
Who stood in silence near his throne, the friends
Of Arthur, gazing on him, tall, with bright
Sweet faces, who will help him at his need.

261 *strait* narrow, strict

266 *Table Round* legends differ about the origin of the famous Round Table. Some say it was made by Merlin for Uther, who gave it to Leodogran, who in turn gave it to Arthur as a wedding present. Others say it was made specially for Arthur by a workman

271–2 *thro' the cross . . .* the sun shining through stained glass windows

274 *vert and azure* green and blue (heraldic terms)

275 *three fair queens* see *Morte d'Arthur* and *Notes*

'And there I saw mage Merlin, whose vast wit
And hundred winters are but as the hands 280
Of loyal vassals toiling for their liege.

'And near him stood the Lady of the Lake,
Who knows a subtler magic than his own—
Clothed in white samite, mystic, wonderful.
She gave the King his huge cross-hilted sword, 285
Whereby to drive the heathen out: a mist
Of incense curl'd about her, and her face
Wellnigh was hidden in the minster gloom;
But there was heard among the holy hymns
A voice as of the waters, for she dwells 290
Down in a deep; calm, whatsoever storms
May shake the world, and when the surface rolls,
Hath power to walk the waters like our Lord.

'There likewise I beheld Excalibur
Before him at his crowning borne, the sword 295
That rose from out the bosom of the lake,
And Arthur row'd across and took it—rich
With jewels, elfin Urim, on the hilt,
Bewildering heart and eye—the blade so bright
That men are blinded by it—on one side, 300
Graven in the oldest tongue of all this world,
"Take me," but turn the blade and ye shall see,

279 *mage* magician and wise man
wit knowledge and wisdom

280–1 Merlin's knowledge and hundred years' experience are at the service of the King.

282 *The Lady of the Lake* see *Notes*

298 *elfin Urim* fairy, or magical, light. Urim and Thummim, mentioned in Exodus and Deuteronomy, were objects worn on the breastplate of the Jewish high priest; Urim was the Hebrew word for lights

And written in the speech ye speak yourself,
"Cast me away!" And sad was Arthur's face
Taking it, but old Merlin counsell'd him, 305
"Take thou and strike! the time to cast away
Is yet far-off." So this great brand the king
Took, and by this will beat his foemen down.'

Thereat Leodogran rejoiced, but thought
To sift his doubtings to the last, and ask'd, 310
Fixing full eyes of question on her face,
'The swallow and the swift are near akin,
But thou art closer to this noble prince,
Being his own dear sister;' and she said,
'Daughter of Gorloïs and Ygerne am I;' 315
'And therefore Arthur's sister?' ask'd the King.
She answer'd, 'These be secret things,' and sign'd
To those two sons to pass, and let them be.
And Gawain went, and breaking into song
Sprang out, and follow'd by his flying hair 320
Ran like a colt, and leapt at all he saw:
But Modred laid his ear beside the doors,
And there half-heard; the same that afterward
Struck for the throne, and striking found his doom.

And then the Queen made answer, 'What know I? 325
For dark my mother was in eyes and hair,
And dark in hair and eyes am I; and dark
Was Gorloïs, yea and dark was Uther too,
Wellnigh to blackness; but this King is fair
Beyond the race of Britons and of men. 330

317 *sign'd* signalled
318 *those two sons* Gawain and Mordred
to pass to go
324 rebelled against the King, and lost his life in the attempt

Moreover, always in my mind I hear
A cry from out the dawning of my life,
A mother weeping, and I hear her say,
"O that ye had some brother, pretty one,
To guard thee on the rough ways of the world." ' 335

'Ay,' said the King, 'and hear ye such a cry?
But when did Arthur chance upon thee first?'

'O King!' she cried, 'and I will tell thee true:
He found me first when yet a little maid:
Beaten I had been for a little fault 340
Whereof I was not guilty; and out I ran
And flung myself down on a bank of heath,
And hated this fair world and all therein,
And wept, and wish'd that I were dead; and he—
I know not whether of himself he came, 345
Or brought by Merlin, who, they say, can walk
Unseen at pleasure—he was at my side,
And spake sweet words, and comforted my heart,
And dried my tears, being a child with me.
And many a time he came, and evermore 350
As I grew greater grew with me; and sad
At times he seem'd, and sad with him was I,
Stern too at times, and then I loved him not,
But sweet again, and then I loved him well.
And now of late I see him less and less, 355
But those first days had golden hours for me,
For then I surely thought he would be king.

'But let me tell thee now another tale:
For Bleys, our Merlin's master, as they say,

336 *and hear ye such a cry?* do you still hear this cry?—i.e., have you found a brother yet?

Died but of late, and sent his cry to me, 360
To hear him speak before he left his life.
Shrunk like a fairy changeling lay the mage;
And when I enter'd told me that himself
And Merlin ever served about the King,
Uther, before he died; and on the night 365
When Uther in Tintagil past away
Moaning and wailing for an heir, the two
Left the still King, and passing forth to breathe,
Then from the castle gateway by the chasm
Descending thro' the dismal night—a night 370
In which the bounds of heaven and earth were lost—
Beheld, so high upon the dreary deeps
It seem'd in heaven, a ship, the shape thereof
A dragon wing'd, and all from stem to stern
Bright with a shining people on the decks, 375
And gone as soon as seen. And then the two
Dropt to the cove, and watch'd the great sea fall,
Wave after wave, each mightier than the last,
Till last, a ninth one, gathering half the deep
And full of voices, slowly rose and plunged 380
Roaring, and all the wave was in a flame:
And down the wave and in the flame was borne
A naked babe, and rode to Merlin's feet,
Who stoopt and caught the babe, and cried "The King!
Here is an heir for Uther!" And the fringe 385
Of that great breaker, sweeping up the strand,
Lash'd at the wizard as he spake the word,

362 *a fairy changeling* usually a child exchanged (by the fairies) for another child. Here simply somebody changed (by the fairies)

379 *a ninth one* so Masefield: 'Send me a ninth great peaceful wave.' Other poets (e.g. Swinburne) maintain that every *third* wave is greater than the others

And all at once all round him rose in fire,
So that the child and he were clothed in fire.
And presently thereafter follow'd calm,
Free sky and stars: "And this same child," he said,
"Is he who reigns; nor could I part in peace
Till this were told." And saying this the seer
Went thro' the strait and dreadful pass of death,
Not ever to be question'd any more
Save on the further side; but when I met
Merlin, and ask'd him if these things were truth—
The shining dragon and the naked child
Descending in the glory of the seas—
He laugh'd as is his wont, and answer'd me
In riddling triplets of old time, and said:

'"Rain, rain, and sun! a rainbow in the sky!
A young man will be wiser by and by;
An old man's wit may wander ere he die.
Rain, rain, and sun! a rainbow on the lea!
And truth is this to me, and that to thee;
And truth or clothed or naked let it be.
Rain, sun, and rain! and the free blossom blows:
Sun, rain, and sun! and where is he who knows?
From the great deep to the great deep he goes."

'So Merlin riddling anger'd me; but thou
Fear not to give this King thine only child,
Guinevere: so great bards of him will sing
Hereafter; and dark sayings from of old
Ranging and ringing thro' the minds of men,
And echo'd by old folk beside their fires
For comfort after their wage-work is done,

401 *of old time* ancient prophecies were often cast in the form of three rhymed lines

Speak of the King; and Merlin in our time
Hath spoken also, not in jest, and sworn
Tho' men may wound him that he will not die, 420
But pass, again to come; and then or now
Utterly smite the heathen underfoot,
Till these and all men hail him for their king.'

She spake and King Leodogran rejoiced,
But musing 'Shall I answer yea or nay?' 425
Doubted, and drowsed, nodded and slept, and saw,
Dreaming, a slope of land that ever grew,
Field after field, up to a height, the peak
Haze-hidden, and thereon a phantom king,
Now looming, and now lost; and on the slope 430
The sword rose, the hind fell, the herd was driven,
Fire glimpsed; and all the land from roof and rick,
In drifts of smoke before a rolling wind,
Stream'd to the peak, and mingled with the haze
And made it thicker; while the phantom king 435
Sent out at times a voice; and here or there
Stood one who pointed toward the voice, the rest
Slew on and burnt, crying, 'No king of ours,
No son of Uther, and no king of ours;'
Till with a wink his dream was changed, the haze 440
Descended, and the solid earth became
As nothing, but the King stood out in heaven,
Crown'd. And Leodogran awoke, and sent
Ulfius, and Brastias and Bedivere,
Back to the court of Arthur answering yea. 445

Then Arthur charged his warrior whom he loved
And honour'd most, Sir Lancelot, to ride forth

423 *these* the heathen

And bring the Queen;—and watch'd him from the
gates:
And Lancelot past away among the flowers,
(For then was latter April) and return'd 450
Among the flowers, in May, with Guinevere.
To whom arrived, by Dubric the high saint,
Chief of the church in Britain, and before
The stateliest of her altar-shrines, the King
That morn was married, while in stainless white, 455
The fair beginners of a nobler time,
And glorying in their vows and him, his knights
Stood round him, and rejoicing in his joy.
Far shone the fields of May thro' open door,
The sacred altar blossom'd white with May, 460
The Sun of May descended on their King,
They gazed on all earth's beauty in their Queen,
Roll'd incense, and there past along the hymns
A voice as of the waters, while the two
Sware at the shrine of Christ a deathless love: 465
And Arthur said, 'Behold, thy doom is mine.
Let chance what will, I love thee to the death!'
To whom the Queen replied with drooping eyes,
'King and my lord, I love thee to the death!'
And holy Dubric spread his hands and spake, 470
'Reign ye, and live and love, and make the world
Other, and may thy Queen be one with thee,
And all this Order of thy Table Round
Fulfil the boundless purpose of their King!'

So Dubric said; but when they left the shrine 475
Great Lords from Rome before the portal stood,
In scornful stillness gazing as they past;

452 *to whom arrived* and to her, when she had arrived. Another Latin form

Then while they paced a city all on fire
With sun and cloth of gold, the trumpets blew,
And Arthur's knighthood sang before the King:— 480

'Blow trumpet, for the world is white with May;
Blow trumpet, the long night hath roll'd away!
Blow thro' the living world—"Let the King reign."

'Shall Rome or Heathen rule in Arthur's realm?
Flash brand and lance, fall battleaxe upon helm, 485
Fall battleaxe, and flash brand! Let the King reign.

'Strike for the King and live! his knights have heard
That God hath told the King a secret word.
Fall battleaxe, and flash brand! Let the King reign.

'Blow trumpet! he will lift us from the dust. 490
Blow trumpet! live the strength and die the lust!
Clang battleaxe, and clash brand! Let the King reign.

'Strike for the King and die! and if thou diest,
The King is King, and ever wills the highest.
Clang battleaxe, and clash brand! Let the King reign. 495

'Blow, for our Sun is mighty in his May!
Blow, for our Sun is mightier day by day!
Clang battleaxe, and clash brand! Let the King reign.

'The King will follow Christ, and we the King
In whom high God hath breathed a secret thing. 500
Fall battleaxe, and flash brand! Let the King reign.'

493 *and if thou diest* and even if thou diest

So sang the knighthood, moving to their hall.
There at the banquet those great Lords from Rome,
The slowly-fading mistress of the world,
Strode in, and claim'd their tribute as of yore. 505
But Arthur spake, 'Behold, for these have sworn
To wage my wars, and worship me their King;
The old order changeth, yielding place to new;
And we that fight for our fair father Christ,
Seeing that ye be grown too weak and old 510
To drive the heathen from your Roman wall,
No tribute will we pay:' so those great lords
Drew back in wrath, and Arthur strove with Rome.

And Arthur and his knighthood for a space
Were all one will, and thro' that strength the King 515
Drew in the petty princedoms under him,
Fought, and in twelve great battles overcame
The heathen hordes, and made a realm and reign'd.

The Revenge

A BALLAD OF THE FLEET

I

At Flores in the Azores Sir Richard Grenville lay,
And a pinnace, like a flutter'd bird, came flying from far away:
'Spanish ships of war at sea! we have sighted fifty-three!'
Then sware Lord Thomas Howard: ''Fore God I am no
coward;
But I cannot meet them here, for my ships are out of gear, 5
And the half my men are sick. I must fly, but follow quick.
We are six ships of the line; can we fight with fifty-three?'

II

Then spake Sir Richard Grenville: 'I know you are no coward,
You fly them for a moment to fight with them again.
But I've ninety men and more that are lying sick ashore. 10
I should count myself the coward if I left them, my Lord Howard,
To these Inquisition dogs and the devildoms of Spain.'

III

So Lord Howard past away with five ships of war that day,
Till he melted like a cloud in the silent summer heaven;
But Sir Richard bore in hand all his sick men from the land 15
Very carefully and slow,
Men of Bideford in Devon,
And we laid them on the ballast down below;
For we brought them all aboard,
And they blest him in their pain, that they were not left to Spain, 20
To the thumbscrew and the stake, for the glory of the Lord.

IV

He had only a hundred seamen to work the ship and to fight,
And he sailed away from Flores till the Spaniard came in sight,
With his huge sea-castles heaving upon the weather bow.
'Shall we fight or shall we fly? 25
Good Sir Richard, tell us now,
For to fight is but to die!
There'll be little of us left by the time this sun be set.'
And Sir Richard said again: 'We be all good English men.
Let us bang these dogs of Seville, the children of the devil, 30
For I never turn'd my back upon Don or devil yet.'

V

Sir Richard spoke and he laugh'd, and we roar'd a hurrah, and so
The little Revenge ran on sheer into the heart of the foe,
With her hundred fighters on deck, and her ninety sick below;

For half of their fleet to the right and half to the left were seen, 35
And the little Revenge ran on thro' the long sea-lane between.

VI

Thousands of their soldiers look'd down from their decks and laugh'd,
Thousands of their seamen made mock at the mad little craft
Running on and on, till delay'd
By their mountain-like San Philip that, of fifteen hundred tons, 40
And up-shadowing high above us with her yawning tiers of guns,
Took the breath from our sails, and we stay'd.

VII

And while now the great San Philip hung above us like a cloud
Whence the thunderbolt will fall
Long and loud, 45
Four galleons drew away
From the Spanish fleet that day,
And two upon the larboard and two upon the starboard lay,
And the battle-thunder broke from them all.

VIII

But anon the great San Philip, she bethought herself and went 50
Having that within her womb that had left her ill content;
And the rest they came aboard us, and they fought us hand to hand,
For a dozen times they came with their pikes and musqueteers,
And a dozen times we shook 'em off as a dog that shakes his ears
When he leaps from the water to the land. 55

IX

And the sun went down, and the stars came out far over the summer sea,
But never a moment ceased the fight of the one and the fifty-three.

Ship after ship, the whole night long, their high-built galleons
came,
Ship after ship, the whole night long, with her battle-thunder and
flame;
Ship after ship, the whole night long, drew back with her dead
and her shame. 60
For some were sunk and many were shatter'd, and so could
fight us no more—
God of battles, was ever a battle like this in the world before?

X

For he said 'Fight on! fight on!'
Tho' his vessel was all but a wreck;
And it chanced that, when half of the short summer night was
gone, 65
With a grisly wound to be drest he had left the deck,
But a bullet struck him that was dressing it suddenly dead,
And himself he was wounded again in the side and the head,
And he said 'Fight on! fight on!'

XI

And the night went down, and the sun smiled out far over the
summer sea, 70
And the Spanish fleet with broken sides lay round us all in a ring;
But they dared not touch us again, for they fear'd that we still
could sting,
So they watch'd what the end would be.
And we had not fought them in vain,
But in perilous plight were we, 75
Seeing forty of our poor hundred were slain,
And half of the rest of us maim'd for life
In the crash of the cannonades and the desperate strife;
And the sick men down in the hold were most of them stark and
cold,

And the pikes were all broken or bent, and the powder was all
of it spent; 80
And the masts and the rigging were lying over the side;
But Sir Richard cried in his English pride,
'We have fought such a fight for a day and a night
As may never be fought again!
We have won great glory, my men! 85
And a day less or more
At sea or ashore,
We die—does it matter when?
Sink me the ship, Master Gunner—sink her, split her in twain!
Fall into the hands of God, not into the hands of Spain!' 90

XII

And the gunner said 'Ay, ay,' but the seamen made reply:
'We have children, we have wives,
And the Lord hath spared our lives.
We will make the Spaniard promise, if we yield, to let us go;
We shall live to fight again and to strike another blow.' 95
And the lion there lay dying, and they yielded to the foe.

XIII

And the stately Spanish men to their flagship bore him then,
Where they laid him by the mast, old Sir Richard caught at last,
And they praised him to his face with their courtly foreign grace;
But he rose upon their decks, and he cried: 100
'I have fought for Queen and Faith like a valiant man and true;
I have only done my duty as a man is bound to do:
With a joyful spirit I Sir Richard Grenville die!'
And he fell upon their decks, and he died.

XIV

And they stared at the dead that had been so valiant and true, 105
And had holden the power and glory of Spain so cheap

That he dared her with one little ship and his English few;
Was he devil or man? He was devil for aught they knew,
But they sank his body with honour down into the deep,
And they mann'd the Revenge with a swarthier alien crew, 110
And away she sail'd with her loss and long'd for her own;
When a wind from the lands they had ruin'd awoke from sleep,
And the water began to heave and the weather to moan,
And or ever that evening ended a great gale blew,
And a wave like the wave that is raised by an earthquake grew, 115
Till it smote on their hulls and their sails and their masts and
their flags,
And the whole sea plunged and fell on the shot-shatter'd navy of
Spain,
And the little Revenge herself went down by the island crags
To be lost evermore in the main.

Crossing the Bar

SUNSET and evening star,
And one clear call for me!
And may there be no moaning of the bar,
When I put out to sea,

But such a tide as moving seems asleep, 5
Too full for sound and foam,
When that which drew from out the boundless deep
Turns again home.

3 *moaning of the bar* the bar is the bank of sand or silt across the entrance to the harbour. At certain states of the tide and wind a 'moaning' sound can be heard above it. Kingsley wrote in the *Three Fishers*, 'though the harbour bar be moaning.'

7–8 *that which drew ...* life, the soul

Twilight and evening bell,
  And after that the dark! 10
And may there be no sadness of farewell,
  When I embark;

For tho' from out our bourne of Time and Place
  The flood may bear me far,
I hope to see my Pilot face to face 15
  When I have crost the bar.

13 *bourne* limit, boundary
15 *my Pilot* Tennyson explained this as 'That Divine and Unseen who is always guiding us'

Notes

TO THE QUEEN

This Dedication was printed at the beginning of the first edition of Tennyson's *Poems* to be published after his appointment as Poet Laureate, which was in fact the seventh edition. It appeared at the beginning of every collected edition thereafter.

MARIANA

In Act 3 Sc. I of *Measure for Measure* the Duke says: 'I will presently to St Luke's; there at the moated grange resides this dejected Mariana.' But the poem owes nothing to Shakespeare's play except the name Mariana, and the 'moated grange'. The sluice (l. 39) and the picture in ll. 41–5 suggest that Tennyson had in mind the strip of level marshland lying between the coast and the Wolds in Lincolnshire.

RECOLLECTIONS OF THE ARABIAN NIGHTS

Tennyson as a young man delighted in painting word-pictures of scenes which were largely imagined—although this is clearly a 'recollection' of a richly-coloured illustration. As an undergraduate he wrote a poem about a 'dark Indian maiden' in Haiti, called *Anacoana*, which was never published but which has many lines and ideas similar to those in this poem.

THE DYING SWAN

The legend of the swan's dying song (which is referred to also in *Morte D'Arthur*) seems to have fascinated classical writers. From Aeschylus and Socrates among the Greeks, through Shakespeare in *King John*, down to Tennyson himself the story persists that the swan, least musical of birds, sings beautifully when it is about to die. Some believe the song to have been doleful; others, like Tennyson, thought it joyful.

THE LADY OF SHALOTT

Tennyson himself said the poem had an allegorical intention. The Lady was content until she saw the 'two young lovers lately wed' (l. 70), but the sight of their happiness disturbed her; so that when she saw 'bold Sir Lancelot' in her mirror and heard him singing she was unable to resist the temptation to look out of her window. Thus the temptations of the world can draw us from the life of contemplation, possibly with fatal results.

To all of which one is tempted to say 'Nonsense'. Whatever the poet himself may have intended, his readers have been content to accept the poem as a delightfully romantic cameo, with no implications beyond the obvious ones. Its setting belongs to the Arthurian world which Tennyson was later to explore so thoroughly, but it is more carefree and less solemn than any of the *Idylls of the King*.

Shalott is another form of Astolat, 'which is Guildford' says Malory (from whom Tennyson derived much of his Arthurian material, though not, apparently, the inspiration for this poem). Camelot is said by some to be in Wales, by others to be Winchester, by others Camel, in Somerset. But if Shalott is Guildford, it is difficult to see how Camelot can be any of these places. The Arthurian map is, to say the least, confused.

ŒNONE

At least a part of this poem was written in the Valley of Cauteretz in the Pyrenees, during the visit mentioned in the *Introduction*, p. 16; but it is full of echoes of descriptive writing from the classics. The story, taken mainly from Ovid, is a sort of footnote to the Trojan wars. Paris, the son of Priam King of Troy and Hecuba his wife, was handed over to a shepherd with instructions to expose him on Mount Ida. The shepherd, however, took him home and brought him up as a country lad. His mother had dreamed, before his birth, that she had borne a firebrand which set fire to the city; when it seemed unlikely that there was anything in the dream Paris was acknowledged by his parents, although he continued to live happily with his wife Œnone, daughter of a river-god, in the mountains. Meanwhile the gods had been attending a feast to celebrate the wedding of Peleus; only one goddess, Eris, had not received an invitation. To show her anger she gate-crashed the feast and threw an apple on the table, inscribed 'For the most fair'. As she was the goddess of Strife she knew quite well what she was doing. Not only did three of the leading ladies of Olympus present rival claims to the apple; the outcome of the dispute led directly to the long and calamitous Trojan wars. Iris, the gods' messenger and herself the goddess of the rainbow, was sent to Paris with the command that he should name the winner of the apple. The three competitors were not above shameless bribery. Herè (or Hera), the Queen of Heaven, offered Paris untold wealth and power; Pallas Athene, goddess of Wisdom, promised infinite wisdom; Aphrodite (the Roman Venus), goddess of Love, offered the most beautiful and most loving wife in Greece. Paris chose Aphrodite, and claimed his reward: Helen, wife of King Menelaus of Sparta, who apparently fitted the description most closely. He went to Sparta and persuaded Helen (whose face thus 'launched a thousand ships') to leave her husband and live with him. The Greeks then went to war with Troy.

Tennyson ends this poem with Œnone's visit to Cassandra, who was a prophetess (and incidentally a sister of Paris), although nobody believed her prophecies. Lines 260 and 261 mention Cassandra's forebodings of the wars to come. In *The Death of Œnone*—one of Tennyson's last poems, which is generally considered much inferior to this—he tells the story to its end. Paris was badly wounded in the war and came to Œnone to be healed; she, not unnaturally, refused to help, and Paris returned to Troy, where he died. Seized with remorse, Œnone hurried after him but arrived too late; so she threw herself into the flames of his funeral pyre.

The place-names are not of major importance. Mount Ida is really a range of mountains in Asia Minor, near to Troy. The Ionian hills were not far away and Gargarus was the southernmost peak of Mount Ida. 'Reedy Simois' was a river rising in Ida. 'Hesperian gold' (l. 65) refers to the Hesperides, mythical islands somewhere in the West, where grew a tree bearing golden apples. 'Idalian' and 'Paphian' (ll. 170–1) refer to towns in ancient Cyprus which were sacred to Aphrodite.

More important than the names is the moral of the poem. Nobody has ever suggested that it is meant to convey anything more than is actually stated, but Pallas Athene's speech (ll. 142–148) is clearly the heart of the poem. It is a noble statement of Tennyson's own beliefs.

THE LOTOS-EATERS

Tennyson took the idea of this poem from the *Odyssey*. On their long homeward journey to Ithaca after the Trojan war, Ulysses and his men touched on an island for water, and the leader sent two men inland to discover what they could of the inhabitants, with a third man as herald. The inhabitants gave the three mariners some of the 'honey-sweet fruit of the lotos' with the result that the men 'had no more wish to bring tidings nor to come back, but there (they) chose to abide with the lotos-eating men, ever feeding on the lotos, and forgetful of (their) homeward way' (*Butcher and Lang*).

The lotos was said by Herodotus to resemble a date in sweetness, and to have been the favourite food of a tribe called the Lotophagi (i.e., lotos-eaters) living on the North African coast.

Like *Œnone*, this poem appeared first in the 1832 collection of Tennyson's poems, but both were considerably revised—and improved—for the 1842 volume. For those who are interested in the workings of the poet's mind and his reactions to unfavourable criticism, extracts from both editions are quoted in, among other works, Stopford Brooke's *Tennyson* (1894).

The first five stanzas are in the Spenserian form which, with its long last line, lends itself admirably to the lazy, slow movement suggested.

OF OLD SAT FREEDOM

Note, in the last two lines, the Tennysonian fear of violence and the assumption that every view which is 'extreme' must also be a 'falsehood'.

YOU ASK ME WHY

The earliest of Tennyson's so-called political poems. He took no active part in politics, and gave his whole allegiance to no party; but the general cast of his political thought was conservative and intensely patriotic. In these verses he seems to contradict himself; after explaining why he chooses to live in England he ends by saying he will 'seek a warmer sky'. This is due to a weakness in the last stanza—a weakness of inexperience, no doubt. What he meant, probably, was that *if* individual freedom ever disappeared (ll. 17–20) from these islands then he *would wish to be* 'wafted from the harbour mouth' *en route for* 'the South'.

The possibility that even in England 'banded unions' might come to 'persecute opinion' and silence 'individual freedom' was not so remote in the 1830's and 1840's as one might at first think. The Reform Bill of 1832 alarmed one section of the population, who saw it as the beginning of the end of privilege; the

Chartists had begun their agitation for still more electoral reform in 1837 and there had been serious rioting; while on the Continent there was a state of uneasy tension following revolts in several countries in the early 1830's. There is no clear evidence to show when *You ask me why* was written; its general tone suggests that its date was probably near that of the preceding set of verses, which was copied out in a letter written by Tennyson in 1834. Both poems appeared for the first time in the 1842 volume.

MORTE D'ARTHUR

The Arthurian legend has attracted writers—and not in England only—since the eighth century; even in the 1950's new versions of it have appeared. The earliest to write about Arthur were the Welsh, and he was at first a king of the fairies. He, or another of the same name, became King of Britain, and fought the Saxons as well as the Picts and Scots. There may even have been two Arthurs, whose stories became blurred and intermingled to form the Arthur who first stands out clearly in Geoffrey of Monmouth's *History of Britain* (twelfth century). Geoffrey's ideas of history were somewhat elastic, and he recorded as fact many things which were almost certainly legendary.

Later writers copied, embroidered, and added to Geoffrey of Monmouth's story; and Sir Thomas Malory (fifteenth century) in his *Morte d'Arthur* set down most of what was known about King Arthur, including a number of other stories which had been added to the canon over the centuries, but which had not previously been very closely associated with him. In Malory's version, Arthur is called on by Rome to pay tribute, but refuses and declares war (see *The Coming of Arthur*). Leaving his kingdom and Guinevere, his wife, in the care of Modred, his nephew, he sets out for Rome, and is about to enter it in triumph when he hears that his nephew has seized Guinevere and the kingdom. He returns to Britain and, in a battle fought in Lyonesse in the far West (usually assumed to be Cornwall), he kills Modred but is himself fatally wounded. The incidents related in Tennyson's poem then follow, and finally Arthur is borne away to Avilion by the three queens—his sister (Queen Morgan le Fay), the Queen of Wales and the Queen of the Waste Lands. For a long time it was seriously believed that Arthur would return from Avilion to lead the Welsh against the English; but a wise abbot of Glastonbury—thought to be Avilion—pretended to discover the tomb of King Arthur in 1189, and 'proved' that the king was quite dead.

Tennyson was first attracted by the Arthurian stories as early as 1830 or so. At one time he planned an epic in twelve books; at a later date he wrote a scenario for a kind of cantata in five acts on the same theme. But for various reasons he abandoned these projects, and did not return to the subject until the 1850's. Meanwhile he had written a few Arthurian poems, among them *The Lady of Shalott* and the *Morte d'Arthur*, the latter appearing for the first time in the 1842 volume. When he had more or less finished his *Idylls of the King*, however, he added about 200 lines to *Morte d'Arthur* and included it as the last *Idyll* (1859).

It has certain affinities with *Œnone*, despite the great difference in subject. Both have many lines of superb poetry, and a few lines of feeble verse; both are capable of an allegorical interpretation. And both have at their heart a passage of vigorous moral teaching, incorporating some of the poet's firm convictions—the speech of Pallas Athene in *Œnone* finding a parallel in Arthur's last speech from the barge.

DORA

This is a typical example of Tennyson's English idylls (he himself spelt them idyls, reserving *idylls* for those of *The King*). They were greatly loved and praised by his contemporaries, and *Dora* at any rate has a certain gentle simplicity which goes some way towards reconciling it with modern taste. We may think it, indeed, *too* simple—and much too sentimental. But it is not to be lightly dismissed. When Tennyson was dealing with real men and women, as opposed to the fictitious characters of his more romantic imagination, he came nearer to true portraiture; the characters of *Dora* and of a few similar poems were no doubt based on people he had known in rural Lincolnshire; and they are recognisable as human beings. Along with the characterisation, moreover, goes a genuine feeling for the English rural atmosphere. The harvest scene in *Dora* is authentic enough; and there is a picture in *Enoch Arden* (a longer poem about simple country people, published a few years later) which brilliantly expresses Tennyson's happy familiarity with village people and their ways:

> Heard and not heard him; as the village girl,
> Who sets her pitcher underneath the spring,
> Musing on him who used to fill it for her,
> Hears and not hears, and lets it overflow.

There is nothing quite comparable in *Dora*, but the poem does bear comparison with Wordsworth's *Michael* in its truth to rural life. *Michael* is, of course, a more detailed picture; but then it is a far longer poem.

AUDLEY COURT

This little idyll, written at Torquay in 1838, represents a different sort of narrative poem; a type of which Tennyson was particularly fond at one period, and which he more or less invented. One or two people, usually cultured, and of the same social standing, entertain each other with elegant conversation or even, as here, with spontaneous songs. As the social level of the characters is higher than that of the characters in a poem like *Dora*, so the language is more elevated.

Tennyson, late in life, wrote of *Audley Court*: 'This poem was partially suggested by Abbey Park at Torquay. Torquay was in old days the loveliest sea village in England and now is a town. In those old days I, coming down from the hill over Torquay, saw a star of phosphorescence made by the buoy appearing and disappearing in the dark sea, and wrote these lines' . . . and then follow the last ten or eleven lines of the poem.

ULYSSES

Tennyson said that this poem 'was written soon after Arthur Hallam's death, and gave my feeling about the need of going forward, and braving the struggle of life, perhaps more simply than anything in *In Memoriam*.' It is generally acknowledged to be the finest short poem of its kind that he wrote. The portrait of the old hero is in itself a masterpiece for a young Englishman of the nineteenth century, himself no more than about twenty-five. There is nothing in Homer about Ulysses in his old age, but Tennyson had no doubt encountered him in Dante:

> No tenderness for my son, nor piety
>   To my old father, nor the wedded love
>   That should have comforted Penelope
>
> Could conquer in me the restless itch to rove
>   And rummage through the world exploring it
>   All human worth and wickedness to prove . . .

Hell. xxvi. 94–99: Dorothy Sayers' translation

Ulysses, the man of vigorous action, provides a striking contrast to the Lotos-Eaters; that one man could have written both poems and made both so convincing is in itself, apart from the sheer poetry, a striking tribute to Tennyson's genius.

LOCKSLEY HALL

In his own lifetime Tennyson found that there were so many efforts to identify the 'I' in this poem with himself that he had to issue a sort of disclaimer. At least two other people (one of them the poet Samuel Rogers) declared that *Locksley Hall* was *their* story. 'The poem,' Tennyson said, 'was a simple invention as to place, incidents and people.' On another occasion, however, he admitted that the place was the Lincolnshire coast.

It is one of the earliest of his attempts to create a character, and one of his most successful. The young man, musing over the home where his lost love dwelt, is the typical young man of his day and of his class—eager, romantic, attracted by the new scientific ideas, driven to a kind of jealous eloquence by disappointed love. Tennyson himself said in later life that this poem, with its sequel, *Locksley Hall, Sixty Years After*, would be among the most significant of his poems historically, since they expressed the tone of the Age at two widely separated points in the 19th century. The vision of the millennium (ll. 127 *et seq.*) occurs several times in Tennyson's work, but he usually placed it at such a remote date in the future that he could have had little real faith in it as a practical solution to the world's troubles.

TITHONUS

In Greek legend Tithonus was a beautiful young prince with whom Aurora, goddess of the Dawn, fell in love. At his request, she granted him the gift of immortality; but as he had not mentioned the matter of eternal youth to go with it, he found that he grew old and decrepit. Moreover his wife Aurora, being a goddess, stayed young and beautiful. Finally her pity overcame her love for him and she changed him into a grasshopper.

The poem was first published in the *Cornhill Magazine* in 1860, but Tennyson himself said that it was 'begun' at the same date as *Ulysses* was written. For this reason, presumably, it is usually printed immediately after the latter poem in the collected works.

A FAREWELL

This poem, says Tennyson's son, was the one 'more especially dedicated to the Somersby stream, and not, as some have supposed, *The Brook*, which is designed to be a brook of the imagination.'

BREAK, BREAK, BREAK

'Made in a Lincolnshire lane at 5 o'clock in the morning between blossoming hedges.' No date is given but it is clearly one of the poems written while the poet was still suffering from the blow of Arthur Hallam's death.

THE POET'S SONG

The significance of this short lyric lies mainly in its last two lines. In *Locksley Hall*, probably written at about the same time, Tennyson 'dipped into the future'; for the most part, however, his poetry has been concerned with the past and the present. Here, however, he states a new theme (for him): the poet 'sings of what the world will be'. Perhaps the strangest part of the statement is that the poet's song about the future was 'gay'.

THE BROOK

Everybody knows *The Brook*—or thinks he does. The lyric, embedded in its simple story, has won universal fame and appreciation; the story has escaped attention. One can imagine Tennyson passing a rueful comment about pearls and mother-of-pearl.

Hallam Tennyson records that the MS of *The Brook* was rescued from the waste-paper basket.

SONGS FROM *THE PRINCESS*

The Princess is a long poem with quite an entertaining story. A young prince, betrothed in childhood to a princess he has never seen, loves her in her portrait. His father sends representatives to claim her and bring her back to fulfil her vows, made on her behalf in her infancy. She rejects them: she has founded a college for young women, which it is death for any man to enter. The Prince and two friends enter the College disguised as women. When they are discovered they are not put to death because the Prince has saved the Princess from drowning, but they are turned out. The Prince's father arrives with an army but open war is avoided. Instead, fifty warriors from the king's army fight a tourney against fifty knights led by the Princess's brothers. The College becomes a hospital for the wounded, among whom are the Prince and his two companions. In nursing the Prince, the Princess falls in love with him and capitulates.

It is potentially, as will be seen—and as Gilbert's *Princess Ida* demonstrated—an amusing story; but it is a dangerous one. For one thing it is liable at any moment to become sentimental; for another, the idea of a ladies' college to which no men may be admitted on pain of death, is itself farcical to modern readers and must have been totally absurd to Tennyson's contemporaries, who still tended to treat women as chattels, and who had certainly never considered seriously the higher education of women. Almost the only way to treat the idea, in fact, would have been half-humorously. With a normal sense of humour Tennyson might have realised that if he wished to plead the cause of the higher education of women, he stood more chance of success by treating the subject as matter for laughter (which is not the same as treating it flippantly) than by presenting it seriously.

However, there *was* a story; and it was sentimental. There was also a great deal of beautiful poetry. So when it was published in 1847 it was reasonably popular, and new editions were called for in 1848, 1850, 1851 and 1853. The *Songs* first appeared in the 1850 edition. Tennyson showed his usual sensitiveness to criticism (and also much commonsense) by alterations and additions in each successive edition; but the fact remains that *The Princess*, for all its undoubted merits, is a poem about a subject which is in itself not fundamentally poetical.

The songs, however, are outside all such criticism. The majority of them were not written specifically for *The Princess*. They were already in Tennyson's note-books and were introduced in the third edition to lighten the general texture of the poem; as he wrote,

> The women sang
> Between the rougher voices of the men,
> Like linnets in the pauses of the wind.

Sweet and low was sent by the poet to his mother together with another lullaby on the same lines, that she might choose which one to publish. Her decision was inevitable; the amazing thing is that the poet himself could ever have considered the alternative (printed by his son in the *Memoir*) in the running for one moment. Both contain the rather sloppy line

> Silver sails all out of the west.

The splendour falls was written in Ireland and records the echoes around Killarney. *Tears, idle tears* was 'written in the yellowing autumn-tide at Tintern Abbey, full for me [Tennyson] of its bygone memories. Few know that it is a blank verse lyric.' The last stanza contains some of the most passionate lines Tennyson wrote. *Come down, O maid* was written in Switzerland and he once called it 'almost his most successful work'—meaning only that in it he had come nearest to what he set out to do. It is not, as the others are, a pure lyric, but part of an idyll which the Princess reads by the bedside of the Prince.

The oddest thing about the *Songs* is that most of them are about love between the sexes or the love of the mother for her child. Why Tennyson thought them suitable for a poem about women who had forsworn marriage and banished men from their presence remains a mystery. He might have been pointing a contrast; he might have had his tongue in his cheek; or he might not have noticed anything strange or inconsistent. We shall never know now!

ODE ON THE DEATH OF THE DUKE OF WELLINGTON

This was published in 1852, on the morning of the Duke's funeral. Tennyson was promised £200 for it—the equivalent of £1,000 today. For some reason it had a bad press, and he offered to forgo part of his fee if the publisher looked like losing money on it. But his sacrifice was not after all necessary. The sales improved, and a second, revised, edition appeared in 1853.

The mixed reception of the *Ode* may possibly have been due to its moments of insincerity—or, more probably, blind hero-worship, since Tennyson was never wilfully insincere. The fact of the matter was that Wellington had outlived a good deal of his popularity. Nobody, even thirty-seven years after Waterloo, wished to detract in the slightest from the Duke's brilliance as a military commander. The public were willing to admit, even, that he had remained a modest, upright, patriotic gentleman. But he should never have entered politics; he was not the first, or the last, to prove that distinction on the battle-field is no qualification for leadership in the councils of state. As Stopford Brooke pointed out, 'he was nothing of a statesman'. As Prime Minister, 'he was first arrogant and afterwards perplexed by the mischief he wrought'. In the excitement over the rejection of the Reform Bill of 1832 his windows had been broken by the mob, and he had been nearly dragged from his horse in the streets of the City. He had even angered many of his own party by agreeing to the emancipation of Roman Catholics.

Neither the public nor the press had forgotten these things, and they objected to Tennyson's indiscriminating praise of the general as a statesman. But there was even more than that for them to complain of. Section VII of the *Ode* shows Tennyson at his most insular, and explains his admiration for the less noble aspects of Wellington and his career. It refers to 'brainless mobs and lawless Powers', for example, and the capital P indicates that Tennyson was not generalising; he was obviously thinking of the one Power which he could never grow to love or admire: France. Poets from Horace to Shakespeare and beyond have hated 'the mob', but by Tennyson's day 'the mob' had begun to resent being called 'brainless' every time it was mentioned. That this was not a passing indiscretion was demonstrated a few lines further on, when Tennyson made it clear that in his view England owed her greatness entirely to 'those great men who fought, and kept it ours'. The millions who were already clamouring for the vote; whose manual labour was contributing to make England free and prosperous; and who had provided the hundreds of thousands of common soldiers and sailors who had served under Wellington and Nelson, were now a force to be reckoned with. The Liberals and Radicals who represented their interests, and who commanded an increasingly influential Press, were not slow to point out that the 'great men' would have been powerless without the solid, inarticulate masses behind them.

Tennyson was hurt and surprised; he had certainly not meant to insult anybody, and had no suspicion that his view was not universally held. Fortunately the *Ode* was, in the end, powerful enough to survive all criticism. The Poet Laureate had a noble subject for his first public celebration and he handled it, on the whole, nobly; but it would have been an even finer poem without Section VII.

THE CHARGE OF THE LIGHT BRIGADE

Probably Tennyson's most famous poem. The Crimean War was a miserable affair by all standards; incompetence on a grand scale, such as was exposed by Florence Nightingale, was balanced by minor blunders like the order given to the Light Brigade of cavalry to charge the massed Russian guns. Who gave the order, and why, is not at this point very important; the order was given, and it was obeyed. Discipline triumphed, as so often in armies of all nationalities in all ages; and the loyal soldiers suffered or died while the incompetents who gave the order went unpunished.

Tennyson shared the national horror at the mistake and the national pride in the soldiers' heroism. His poem was published in December 1854 in a newspaper. 'The criticism of two or three London friends' induced him to remove the suggestion that 'someone (i.e., an important personage in society circles) had blundered'; but it is to his credit that he quickly recanted and restored the line to its place in the poem. In response to a demand from the battle-front Tennyson had a thousand copies of the poem printed and distributed to the troops in the Crimea.

FLOWER IN THE CRANNIED WALL

In this moving fragment Tennyson is trying to express what he called 'an universal apologue'; i.e., a fable or allegory with a lesson for all mankind. In a letter to a friend about it he wrote: 'I may remark that you have fallen into a not uncommon error with respect to my little fable . . . as if "I" in the poem meant A. T. and "the flower" my own verses.' There seems little reason to interpret 'the flower' as meaning Tennyson's 'own verses', but if the 'I' of the poem is *not* Tennyson, then the poem loses half its force. It expresses much of the doubt and rather sorrowful bewilderment which is characteristic of Tennyson's religious poetry, and it is difficult to see why he should have been reluctant to own up to it. (He might more profitably have explained why he used a singular verb with a plural subject in the last line!)

IN MEMORIAM

If proof were needed that *In Memoriam* was a collection of separate elegies, and was not conceived as one continuous poem, it could be found in the fact that it is possible to isolate ten of the sections, as in this *Selection*, without doing grave injustice either to the poet or to *In Memoriam*. Admittedly these isolated elegies are seen to greater advantage when read in their context, but even when read separately they have power and beauty.

The introduction, or prologue, was written in 1849 when the whole collection was being prepared for the press. It is in some ways a summary of the whole work and might have made a fitting epilogue. However, Tennyson, with that strange lack of self-criticism which descends on even the greatest artists at some time, added an epilogue which is in every way vastly inferior to everything else in *In Memoriam*, and is utterly out of place.

Section XI is one of a sequence in which Tennyson follows, from his home in Lincolnshire, the progress of Hallam's body from Trieste, where it was placed on a ship, to the Church of St Andrew at Clevedon in Somerset where it was buried in January 1834. The Hallam family lived at Clevedon Court.

Section XIX was written at Tintern Abbey, on the Wye. Sections XXVIII and XXX were written near, if not actually at, Somersby. The word 'gambol'd' is perhaps an odd choice for the kind of games one imagines being played in the Tennyson circle, but it will be remembered that there were still young people about the house. The poet's youngest brother was fifteen in 1834, and his youngest sister seventeen. For their sakes at least, the Christmas games would be played; but for the older members of the family 'the awful sense Of one mute Shadow watching all' must have been distressing. A rainy Christmas apparently added to the general gloom.

Section LIV is from a sequence in which Tennyson tries to derive comfort and inspiration from his faith; and although he seems to fail we feel that he has drawn strength from the very effort. It was this apparently *unsuccessful* effort to find complete healing in religious faith which did so much to endear *In Memoriam* to his readers; had he succeeded and found all the rest and solace which every mourner seeks he would have placed himself by that much above the majority of ordinary people, who have also failed to find the perfect peace which they were seeking, but who have not therefore lost faith.

Section LXXXVI was written at Barmouth, in West Wales, probably in 1839. Section CVI, however, some twenty sections further on, was probably written in January 1838, a year earlier. This is an additional illustration of the patch-work nature of *In Memoriam*. By this time the Tennysons had moved to High Beech, in Epping Forest, and the obviously woodland setting of Section CXV suggests that that also was written at High Beech, a few months after CVI.

THE COMING OF ARTHUR

The Arthurian legend in its journeys from North Britain and Wales, via Brittany and France and England, and back to Wales, acquired a vast number of variants, alternatives and inconsistencies. Malory incorporated most of the variants in his great *Morte d'Arthur*, on which Tennyson drew liberally, but Tennyson added still more. The story told by Bellicent of Arthur's coronation is Tennyson's invention, and is introduced for a purpose.

Although *The Coming of Arthur* was not written—or at any rate published—until four of the *Idylls of the King* had appeared, it must be regarded as the introduction to the series. As the *Idylls* grew in number, and as Tennyson pondered the collection as a whole, it became obvious that a moral and allegorical thread was making itself felt. Whether the poet intended this from the first is not quite clear, but certainly by the time he came to write this poem in the series he had begun to see Arthur less and less as a king, and more and more as a symbol. It was the same with the knights, even with the Round Table itself. In the Arthurian legend they are all parts of a great legend of chivalry and knight-errantry; in the *Idylls* they are all parts of a great allegory; they stand for chastity, for obedience, for loyalty, and so on. In the separate idylls all the characters except Arthur himself and one or two minor ones depart from this ideal, but that doesn't alter the fact that in the beginning they were not mortal men and women, as they were in the original legends, but little more than labelled abstractions. To establish this position Tennyson had to bring in the panoply and the incense of Arthur's coronation, at which all the vows which went to make up these ideal knights were first sworn. He carries the symbolism even further. The Lady of the Lake (l. 282, etc.) is herself a symbol of the Church—but she is also one of the women in the funeral barge in his *Morte d'Arthur*.

By writing his introduction half-way through, so to speak, Tennyson also had the advantage of scattering hints concerning other parts of the series. Knowing, for example, that Lancelot and Guinevere were subsequently to prove unfaithful to Arthur, we nod wisely when we read in *The Coming of Arthur* about the king's love for Lancelot and about his sending of Lancelot to bring Guinevere from her father's court. When we read in this poem about Excalibur our minds immediately turn to *Morte d'Arthur*; just as we contrast the ship 'bright with a shining people on the decks' (l. 375) which brought Arthur, with the barge 'dense with stately forms / Black-stoled, black-hooded' which bore him away in *Morte d'Arthur*.

All this helps to build up, not to destroy, our respect for Tennyson. Critics have complained about the slow narration of some of the *Idylls*; they have deplored the unreality of the characters, especially that of Arthur himself, and wished that Tennyson had either stuck to Malory and written plain tales without a moral, or had concentrated on the ideals and written a straightforwardly moral poem. There is much weight in these criticisms of course, and modern opinion is that, on the whole, the *Idylls of the King* was not the masterpiece his contemporaries thought it. But within the limits Tennyson set himself the work was not unsuccessful. He skilfully interwove what he took from Malory with what he contributed himself; when it suited his purpose, in fact, as with the rival stories of Merlin and of Bleys, he combined different versions of the same incident; and the result, if it is not always convincing, is always interesting. The verse, moreover, compels admiration. Sometimes it may seem a little heavily weighted with Latinisms, but it is seldom obscure; and one reads expectantly, knowing that every now and then a flash of pure poetry, a vivid picture, a masterly turn of speech will occur, to bring us up short with delight and wonder. Even the blank verse in which the poem is written is some of the finest to be found in Tennyson—in places, in fact, some of the finest to be found in the language, outside Shakespeare

THE REVENGE

Hallam Tennyson writes, in his *Memoir*: 'The line, "At Florès in the Azorès Sir Richard Grenville lay," was on my father's desk for years, but he finished the ballad at last all at once in a day or two.' The poem was published in the *Nineteenth Century* in March 1878. Tennyson got his material from Froude, the historian, and from the archives of the Hakluyt Society. In fact only fifteen of the Spanish fleet of 53 vessels actually fought the *Revenge*, but this does not, of course, lessen the glory. Nor does the fact that Grenville was a tough, savage commander, who was reputed to chew glass until the blood poured from his mouth.

CROSSING THE BAR

This was written in 1889, when the poet was over eighty, 'on a day in October' says his son, 'when we came from Aldworth to

Faringford'. Aldworth was his home in Surrey and Faringford his home in the Isle of Wight. 'Before reaching Faringford he had the Moaning of the Bar in his mind, and after dinner he showed me the poem written out.'

At Tennyson's own wish this poem is put at the end of every edition of his complete works. Nobody will doubt the old man's judgement. The quiet optimism seems to be a solution of all the doubts which had troubled him throughout his life; but in addition there is the sound of the sea in it, and the sea had been one of his great loves.